FOR REFERENCE

AFRICAN AMERICANS -- ANALYSIS, BEHAVIOR, PROGRESS AND RESULTS: INDEX OF NEW INFORMATION AND GUIDE-BOOK FOR CONSUMERS, REFERENCE AND RESEARCH

ABBE RESEARCH DIVISION

THE WORLD'S BEST REFERENCE & RESEARCH BOOKS

FIRST EDITION

ABBE PUBLISHERS ASSOCIATION OF WASHINGTON, D.C.

E-MAIL: abbe.publishers@verizon.net

Fax or Telephone: (703) 642-5966

REFERENCE: BOWKER'S "BOOKS IN PRINT"
CATALOG: BOWKER'S "BOOKS IN PRINT"

ISBN: 07883-1484X

BE AN EXPERT WITH ABBE INDEXES

ABBE PUBLISHERS: PROFESSIONAL INFORMATION

I.S.B.N. ASSIGNMENTS: 0-941864; 0-88164; 1-55914; 0-7883+

THIS VOLUME: HARDCOVER EDITION: ISBN: 07883-1484X

THIS VOLUME: PAPERBACK EDITION: ISBN: 07883-14955

COPYRIGHTS 2004, 2003 2002, 2001, 2000, 1998, 1996, 1994, 1992, 1990, 1988, 1986, 1984, 1982, 1980, 1978, 1976, 1974, 1972, 1970.
OF: ABBE PUBLISHERS ASSOCIATION OF WASHINGTON, D.C.
ALL RIGHTS RESERVED. MANUFACTURED IN THE U.S.

SPECIAL NOTATION:
WE CONTINUE TO OBEY REQUESTS FOR GENEROUS SPACING ALLOTMENTS TO PERMIT RESEARCH PHYSICIANS, SCIENTISTS, PIONEERS, LABS AND GRADUATE STUDENTS TO INSERT NOTES, DISCOVERIES, NEW DATA AND CURRENT OR NEW REFERENCES TO MAINTAIN THEIR LOGS OF NEW MATERIAL FOR COPYRIGHTS, POSSIBLE PATENTS AND APPLIED TECHNOLOGIES AS WELL AS PROCEDURAL PROTOCOL FOR MASTER'S THESES AND DOCTORAL DISSERTATIONS.

LIBRARY OF CONGRESS CATALOG CARD NUMBER
LIBRARY OF CONGRESS CATALOGING IN PUBLICATION DATA
<>ABBE INDEX & REFERENCE BOOKS ARE FAR BEYOND TEXTBOOKS
AND CAN BE ADDED TO YOUR ARCHIVES.

FIRST EDITION
FEBRUARY 2002

```ALL ABBE BOOKS AND MONOGRAPHS may be ordered instantly from Baker & Taylor Books, Blackwell's Book Services, Amazon, Com, Barnes & Noble, Borders Books & Music, The Book House, Academic Book Center, Eastern Book Co, Yankee Book Peddler, Emery-Pratt Co. and many others as listed in Library Reference Sources.

*WRITE TO:  ABBE PUBLISHERS ASSOCIATION OF WASHINGTON, D.C.
VIRGINIA DIVISION: 4111 GALLOWS ROAD,   ANNANDALE, VA 22003

==================================================================
INTERNET VISIT: SEE OUR CATALOG IN BOWKER'S "BOOKS IN PRINT"
==================================================================

E-MAIL: abbe.publishers@verizon.net      PHONE OR FAX (703) 642-5966

ABBE PUBLISHERS PRODUCES BOOKS OF NEW INFORMATION
AND NEW KNOWLEDGE FOR WORLD PROGRESS IN ALL NATIONS

MEDICAL RESEARCH PRODUCES NEW KNOWLEDGE, PROLONGS LIFE, INCREASES OUR HAPPINESS, FIGHTS NEW AND OLD DISEASES, LESSENS THE WEARINESS OF LIFE AND ALWAYS SEEKS GREATER PROTECTION AND BETTER HEALTH FOR OUR PRICELESS CHILDREN -- "THE FLOWERS OF CIVILIZATION" (JCB).

**\*\*VISIT ABBE CATALOG IN BOWKER'S  "BOOKS IN PRINT"**

**.....BE AN EXPERT WITH ABBE INDEXES....**
```

TABLE OF CONTENTS

```
r 610 A258 2004
African Americans : analysis
behavior, progress and resul
: index of new information a
```

1. TITLE - 1
2. PUBLISHER INFORMATION - 3
3. PREFACE ONE - 5
4. PREFACE TWO - JUST FOR YOU ! - 7
5. THE GREAT IMPORTANCE OF RESEARCH FOR YOU   9
6. DEDICATION AND REMEMBRANCE - 11
7. PROLOGUE AND SOME PHILOSOPHY - 13
8. ** CONNECTING YOU TO WORLD RESEARCH >>>>>>>> 14
9. LARGER TYPE FOR TIRED SCIENTISTS' EYES   15
10. ACKNOWLEDGMENTS - 16
11. INTRODUCTION : 17
    A. THE IMPORTANCE OF RESEARCH ON EARTH
    B. THE IMPORTANCE OF REFERENCES, INDEXES AND ALL BIBLIOGRAPHIES
    C. SURVIVAL MEANS "PUBLISH OR PERISH!"
       (Stay ahead of deterioration, decay and disease)
       (Survival means research is of great importance)
        1. THE UNSEEN PRIVATE GHOSTLY WARS OF RESEARCH, SCIENTISTS AND LIBRARIANS
12. INDEX OF AUTHORS, SUBJECTS AND MODERN RESEARCH CATEGORIES - 21
13. BIBLIOGRAPHICAL REFERENCES - 122
14. EPILOGUE -AND FARE--THEE--WELL! - 199

<< WE MAKE PROGRESS FOR ALL NATIONS >>

"NEW INFORMATION BEYOND ALL TEXTBOOKS"

VISIT ABBE CATALOG IN BOWKER'S "BOOKS IN PRINT"

AT THE END:
YOUR CATALOG OF NEW AND RECENT BOOKS

"BE AN EXPERT WITH ABBE INDEXES...."

GENERAL PREFACE AND SOME PHILOSOPHY

ABBE PUBLISHERS serves science and medicine for mankind in general and specifically for doctors, scientists, medical graduates, biologists, personnel in all technologies and for those aspiring intellects seeking pioneer challenges, new avenues for research and any kind of improvement to put into laboratory, clinical or emergency practice now. The ten leading causes of death in the U.S. create 20 million casualties a year. We have millions more in lame, sickness, disabled in mind and body with the accoutrements of depression, despair and loss of courage and hope. There is unlimited research work for everybody.

Anyone interested in prevention of death, disease, disasters or sickness can easily find important information, new research topics, references, authors and new or rare publications in our published volumes. These monographs as texts serve as REFERENCE BOOKS, RESEARCH INDEXES & RESEARCH GUIDE-BOOKS as well as collected REVIEWS providing the latest of the best research. These professional texts save considerable time and effort in search, study, survey or examination of your special interests or need as well as promotion of knowledge and advancements for mankind.

We specialize in all matters pertaining to HEALTH; WHAT ARE WE WITHOUT GOOD HEALTH. Yet, the world and civilization greatly neglects health care -as proven by the direful absence of health promotion, health maintenance and metabolic balance. Health is still not a world number one priority. How sad. Try to imagine seeking an occupation, love or happiness while in poor health.

These monographs are important to all professions because they represent an UP-TO-DATE INFORMATION SERVICE, NEW RESEARCH COVERAGE AND PROFESSIONAL ANALYSIS of whatever progress is evolving in research. These monographs also serve as a spear for progress into unknown realms.

Librarians, Library Specialists, Library scientists and Information Advisors have these monographs and research books at their disposal whenever they wish to direct doctor or student to special sources for depth and research promise of success. These reference books also give valuable service to all counselors of professions, guidance personnel, professors, research directors, experimental scientists and clinical investigators. Supervisors give these monographs and research indexes to their graduate students to search for THESIS TOPICS. This material adds value and speed to research grant applicants. DISSERTATION topics are easily found in ABBE BOOKs for pioneer research and graduate degrees.

Reference Indexes, Research Monographs, Medical Reviews, Guide-books of Research and Subject Survey Analyses all have their place in the history of field development. These books are a hallmark of the professions and serve as an emblem of progressive research for all mankind.

*EVERYONE MUST HELP IN OUR BATTLES AGAINST SICKNESS AND ALL DISEASES
WHICH ARE QUIETLY WAITING FOR US....

PREFACE TWO - MADE FOR YOU!

Readers not acquainted with fields of science or medicine need not worry or feel intimidated by reading medical or any science articles in any journal. Such literature offers small disadvantage --that of becoming acquainted with the vocabulary therein. This you can do by diligent use of a dictionary to identify the terms used in the articles of your interest or pursuit. Once this is done you have made significant progress.

Learning the limited vocabulary in journal articles gives you a wondrous view of the subject. Hiring a consultant would have been wasteful and expensive. Instead you've done the work by yourself, thus saving time and money and without appointment or disappointment.

Authors of research publications listed herein are important. One often wonders what else this author-scientist-physician may have published, or possess still new but unpublished research. These indexes list all authors so often you will find the same author listed more than once, indicating other publications of this author that may expand your interest or range of intent.

When you find an article you should notice the location of the author and listed address. In times of great need you can write directly to such authors -as in severe illness, near-death scenes or request more new data for a thesis or dissertation degree.

In your literature-subject search, by foot, computer or internet be sure to locate review articles first. Reviews are packed with new data, methods, summaries, controversies and conclusions. They present a sum condensation of years of research in a nutshell for you. You can select and carry research on from there --and becoming a 'new' pioneer!

Intellectually, this civilization is still quite primitive: less than .1% of all people are involved in research -while new diseases as HIV and AIDS creep up on us. Our Indexes help overcome this severe deficit and lead you directly into new discoveries.

HEALTH CARE IS YOUR BEST PRIORITY OF LIFE.
THE GREAT IMPORTANCE OF RESEARCH

FOR YOU AND THE WORLD*

1. Nations or citizens without new knowledge, research or arms for health and self-defense become the prey they deserve.
   [Reminder: The law of the Jungle always pertains]

2. Nations without research progress become easy, early victims of disease.

3. Many of us today would not be alive but for antibiotic research.

4. New research prolongs life, health and happiness too.

5. Without new research wars would be always raging somewhere.

6. Research seeks the Holy Grail of heavenly Utopia for mankind.

7. Research is the beating heart of progress for health and longevity.

8. The status of nations is easily determined by their research production.

9. Where there is less research there is more poverty, illness and disease.

10. Research helps babies survive birth & early childhood.

11. Creativity demands constant feeding of new information.

12. Research is the secret gold-mine for civilization.

13. Research is the best offense and defense against any kind of creeping illness, unknown diseases and causes of early deaths.

14. Graduate school research is a wonderful cauldron of and for creativity.

15. The best universities have highly productive research scientists.

16. Research gives great rewards, fame or cheerful life satisfaction.

17. The best students come from highly motivated teachers & scientists.

18. Rapid research promotes publication of Reference Books & Research Indexes: sources of new information beyond current textbooks.

19. Synthesis of new information creates New Knowledge for Progress.

* Excerpts from the book: "Health, Life & Disease Or Why Research Should Be Of Great Importance To All Governments, Consumers, Community leaders, Military Chiefs, Civic and Civilian Leaders, Cosmopolitans and Librarians: A philosophy of life made simple. Dr. John C. Bartone. Abbe Publishers. HC: ISBN 0-7883-1034-6; PB: 1025-4
U.S. COPYRIGHT 1995: ABBE PUBLISHERS & DR. BARTONE. ALL RIGHTS RESERVED.

DEDICATION AND REMEMBRANCE

REMEMBER THE LOST,

BEAT,

TORTURED,

SOLD,

NEGLECTED

AND

ENSLAVED

SOULS

BY A

MINDLESS MANKIND

AND AN

IGNORANT CIVILIZATION.

PROLOGUE AND SOME PHILOSOPHY

NO ONE SEEMS TO CONSIDER

THAT

AFRICAN AMERICANS

HAVE THEIR OWN

CONTINUAL HOLOCAUST

WHICH IS NOT

PROPERLY RECORDED,

AS WELL AS

HISTORICALLY IGNORED,

CONSIDERED AS AN

'IRRELEVANT INCIDENT'

IN AMERICAN-NATIONAL PROGRESS

AND, OF COURSE,

NEVER GIVEN SERIOUS THOUGHT

FOR MORAL, LEGAL

OR

MONETARY COMPENSATION

FOR THE ENDLESS PAIN

OF THE DENIAL OF SUCH

HOLOCAUST TREATMENT.

CONNECTING YOU TO WORLD RESEARCH, INFORMATION AND NEW KNOWLEDGE PRODUCED BY ALL NATIONS

Planet Earth is not an intellectual planet. Its civilization and scattered populations are devoid of high priority protocols, as for example,
1. NO complete health care for everyone.
2. NO total and special care for newborn and infants;
3. NO logical, disciplinary education for all adolescents;
4. NO compulsory training programs for all students.
5. NO genetic testing to help citizens obtain a good life;
6. NO basic 10 laws for living a good, organized life;
7. NO display of a good, clean, honest government;
8. NO guidance for the necessity of research -without which there can be no better life for mankind;
9. NO UNIVERSAL LAW: ONE AND ALL MUST PERFORM RESEARCH THROUGH-OUT THEIR LIVES;
10. NO constant, continual support for ALL scientists – the pioneers endowed to save mankind.

RESEARCH on Planet Earth today is a hap-hazard process in all nations. Research is a vast ocean of negligence: its international aggregate production is a combined .5%. Disease, ignorance, evil politics and parasites, among others, control Planet Earth.

Much research produced has no bearing –or connection -- to the heap of information and knowledge in existence. 60% of published articles have no references or bibliography! There are many reasons for this, but none are truly valid. All research must be connected to the "hills" of old and current knowledge stored everywhere.

Research citations are omitted for many reasons, to reduce cost, space and other factors. They may be ignored due to conceit, fraud, malpractice, commerce or peer dominance; whatever.

Research production of Indexes, Encyclopedias, Reference Works, Reviews and Bibliographies are of crucial importance: they quickly connect anyone to what we already know–or to seek help, such as to save Life, Health -or our "children- the flowers of civilization".
How long can this civilization survive without much good research?

LARGER TYPE FOR TIRED SCIENTISTS' EYES

ABBE Index and Reference books get much close attention and use with continual referral back again and again to different pages of text, the indexes or the bibliographies for the services they provide. This is especially true when sorting or comparing different authors and their research papers. Some have citations in their work and many others do not. As a further result many other complications arise when some authors offer a few citations and other writers working in the same field or area list many more citations.

The general consequence therefore is that much more reading and pouring over citations is required. Most journals and articles place citations at the end of the research papers and are presented in very small type. Thus, reading citations in science and medical journals is an eye-burning strain and squinting task.

Aging eyes, people beginning the 'bifocal stage' quickly begin to have difficulty reading small-point citations. Worse, most scientists, technicians, collaborators, directors and other scientific and medical personnel, with aging eyes, over 40, do not always keep a 20/20 vision. Many do of course, by the frequent change of eyeglasses. But in all lives, there are periods when reading small type is not readily achieved.

We have always claimed that important papers, -of any kind - should be in larger type. As we age, we should find it easier and more enjoyable to read larger printed works. Unfortunately, with dismay, such accommodation is not given due to labor and costs. However, these Indexes and Reference books are meeting the needs of tired and aging eyes -so that scientists, physicians and collaborators may easily and rapidly read our books and continue to contribute research for the benefit of mankind.

CITATIONS ARE NECESSARY. THEY RULE THE RESEARCH WORLD

ABBE INDEXES GIVE QUICK EXPERTISE

"CITATIONS CONNECT YOU TO OLD AND NEWLY FOUND KNOWLEDGE"

ACKNOWLEDGMENTS

We are grateful and indebted to many professional and technical workers and personnel in all parts of the biomedical world. There would be no end to the list of those individuals who should be named as public acknowledgment of their help, guidance, courtesy and even professional rescue at times. We are also appreciative of guidance to leading research physicians and scientists who work without public acclaim and without public gratitude.

These generous and devoted people are certainly a contribution to the world of progress all nations and civilization so desperately need against the constant struggle and battles against poverty, disease and disabling illnesses.

We also wish to thank the many government departments, agencies and federal employees at all levels for their ever so diligent application of time and energy as we strive to help mankind survive with increase of health and happiness.

Many thanks must also be extended to the Directors and Staff of the Library of Medicine for their prodigious productions of the many volumes of biomedical information, services and data resources.

The titles of articles in translation, often used here as well as all over the world, have been performed by the specialists of the Library and to them we happily give full credit.

The Staff of the Library of Congress, the LC Card Catalog personnel and the Cataloging in Publication (CIP) Divisions, full of rare patience of the enduring kind, have always been exceedingly courteous and professional in their services. They also are a national asset of great worth for all mankind.

INTRODUCTION

A. THE IMPORTANCE OF RESEARCH ON EARTH

A rule of the universe is prevalent, unrelenting deterioration, degradation and decay. This action pertains to everything, organic, inorganic, plant, animal or mineral. All is downward transformation. Therefore we must strive to save, improve, invent, manufacture or create the necessities to maintain what we have, what we are or what we need for health, happiness and longevity. This can be accomplished by research to prevent our sliding backward into early death and oblivion. In brief this process is described by the well-known "PUBLISH OR PERISH" slogan. There is infinitesimal awareness in the general world population of "publish or perish"; yet it is an absolute rule of life that governs us all, knowingly or not.

B. THE IMPORTANCE OF REFERENCES, INDEXES, REVIEWS AND ALL BIBLIOGRAPHIES.

These resources are the details of research and help form the stable building blocks of progress for science, medicine, you, your family and all nations.

Survival of self, nations, civilizations and of the world entails many basic ingredients among which the gain, care and use of new knowledge is the principle of intellectual life and progress. The attention, feeding and correct assimilation of new information is gaining increasing 'neglect', concern and dissipation*. There still is no broad, correct spectrum of uniform advance of new data or its application in a continuous, steady and comprehensive manner -as an army marching to its objectives in organized units and goals**. At best, it can be said that bibliographies and reference works lie about as weeds in a dense jungle of loose information including, in these modern times, computerized data.

Librarians are the guiding lights of knowledge to information storage of vast dimension, research guidance and as counselors to student inquires of rare and unknown subjects. Librarians are entrusted with the rare and holy wars of all time: to amass all matter pertinent to health and our survival and progress from a to z. Life is war and they know it well. Librarians are among the few that understand the necessity, importance and the collection of many sorts and manners of reference material be it in whatever style or diversity for its contents may be eventually in great demand, need or consequence at any time--unexpectedly or otherwise.

Wars have a habit of making old research a national crisis. When World War II began we lost our supply of rubber. Our old chemistry of (neglected) research archives, with new knowledge, permitted synthetic development of substitutes of rubber--and a winning war.

World War II forced us to invent research to produce synthetic quinine which prevented malaria. This rapid research saved many American GIs in the Pacific campaigns (which included some of ABBE's old scientist-authors). Thus, data, old or new, is important.

Reference books, as librarians, also serve as guides in enduring struggles to promote progress for mankind. Reference works, any species thereof, aid, lift and nurture the seeds of human aspiration for creativity for those so able and endowed to seek and explore -
and publish --advancements --for country and civilization.

All disciplines, as medical and health, require ultra-new sources of information, especially in presentable form for rapid work, use and assimilation, be it vital or otiose. We have done this for many years.

Scientists are dependent upon librarians to save time, money and energy in literature searches. Our tomes are designed to aid these expectations and prevent engulfment from the tidal waves of world journals presenting and publishing scatter-shot data varieties.

Graduate work of all ages and subjects requires the best books and reference sources. Shortages of reference books and indexes is easily demonstrated: much modern graduate work, theses and dissertations reveal a "re-hash" of known data and information. Symptoms are everywhere; causes are easily diagnosed.

The design, foresight and presentation of ABBE Reference Books and Indexes solves unnecessary need of "rehash". ABBE books offer suggestions for new research for whatever project in demand. These books are marks of world advancements for today and as an emblem of local, national or international progress for tomorrow.

C. PUBLISH OR PERISH !

Nations or individuals that do not create new and publish research indicates a presence of overwhelming problems, as stagnation, a lack of priorities, a miring in the progress of yester-years. Without creativity and publishing new things, deterioration hastens our degeneration. It is not a surprise to us that few people live to a healthy and happy old age! Little, none or slight research means less health care, more child deaths and disease invitations to all.

Life and happiness, with fine health of course, is never, or ever constant --or always good. The seven stages of man reveal man's rainbow of life --with all the infinite problems of neglected health and invading disease. We must teach everyone to learn how to make new contributions to life, society and the world, no matter how small. A mighty mass of new information is constantly needed to make better our life, health, happiness, love, creature comforts and longevity too.

We still have not eliminated wars, diseases, child abuse, drug misuse, unhappy marriages, sufferings of all types, mental illness, poor health, rampart cancers, universal mal-nutrition, pollution everywhere, poisons and contaminations of food. World populations remain mostly immature. The psyche of man and child is too much neglected. Absence of much needed research progress is anywhere in all peoples and nations. Thus our mission: to produce ultra-new Reference Works, Indexes and Guide-Books. Further, we promote the protection and maintenance of your health and peace of mind.

*Health, Life and Disease --Or Why Research Should Be Of Great Importance to All Governments, Consumers, Community Leaders, Military Chiefs, Civic and Civilian Pioneers, Cosmopolitans and Librarians: A Philosophy of Progress Made Simple. Dr. John C. Bartone. ABBE Publishers Association of Washington, D.C. 3rd Printing. January 2000. Hardcover: ISBN 0-7883-1424-6; Pb: 1023-2.

INDEX OF NEW INFORMATION OF PUBLISHED RESEARCH: AUTHORS, SUBJECTS, RESEARCH CATEGORIES AND BIBLIOGRAPHICAL REFERENCES

NOTE

THE NUMBER FOLLOWING EACH CATEGORY REFERS YOU TO THE SAME NUMBER LISTED AS A REFERENCE TITLE IN THE BIBLIOGRAPHY.

INDEXES ARE A FAST INTRODUCTION
AND
CONNECTION
TO
WHAT'S NEW
IN THE
WORLD OF HUMAN RESEARCH

"BE AN EXPERT WITH ABBE INDEXES..."

A PROSTATE PREDICTOR: URINARY SYMPTOMS
182.

A REVIEW: ORGAN-TISSUE DONATION
170.

DISPARITIES, RACIAL, IN CHRONIC HEART DISEASE AND MORTALITY 168.

HIV-AIDS SYNDROME CRISIS
195.

ORGAN DONATION: PROBLEM AND SOLUTION
170.

RACE AND POLITICS OF ABANDONMENT: N.Y.C.
169.

SAFE MOTHERHOOD USA
181.

1990-1997: LOS ANGELES HIV-AIDS WOMEN
177.

1995 SURVEY; ALCOHOL AND DRIVING
189.

21ST CENTURY: PROSTATE CANCER DETECTION
180.

A MILLION VOICES FOR HEALTH CARE
003.

ABANDONMENT, POLITICS OF, IN N.Y. CITY
169.

ABNORMAL EATING ATTITUDES
005.

ABUSE, COCAINE; TREATMENTS FOR
106.

ABUSE DURING PREGNANCY
006.

ABUSE, SEXUAL; CHILDHOOD; EFFECTS OF
145.

ACHIEVEMENT: PERCEPTIONS, ATTITUDES
098.

ACTIVATION OF CONFLICTING STEREOTYPES
187.

ACTIVITY, PHYSICAL: MEASUREMENT: WOMEN
083.

ADDICTION AND TREATMENT: COCAINE
051.

ADDICTS, WORKING: ECONOMICS & SUB USE
193.

ADJUSTMENT, CHILD
172.

ADJUSTMENT TO MASTECTOMY
096.

ADOLESCENT CIGARETTE SMOKING
178.

ADOLESCENT MINORITY MOTHERS & SEX ABUS
145.

ADOLESCENT WELL-BEING IN DISADVANT FAM
075.

ADOLESCENT: TREATMENT DIFFERENCES
108.

ADOLESCENTS IN HIGH-RISK ENVIRONMENTS
011.

ADOLESCENTS IN PUBLIC HOUSING & CONDOMS
011.

ADOLESCENTS, STD, HIV & PREGNANCY PREV
132.

ADOLESCENTS, US: SMOKING: RACE, INCID
110.

ADOLESCENTS: SOCIAL INTERACTIONS
060.

ADOLESCENTS' USE OF PRENATAL CARE
052.

ADOPTION DEBATE: TRANS-RACIAL
057.

ADROGUE HJ ET AL
127.

ADULTS, HOSPITALIZED; RACIAL DIFFERENCES
166.

ADULTS: INJECTING DRUG USE & SCHOOL D-O
191.

ADVERSE 5-YEAR OUTCOME AFTER BYPASS S
008.

AFFIRMATIVE ACTION POLITICS
009.

AFR-AM & WHITES: A METABOLIC SYNDROME
079.

AFR0-AMERICAN WOMEN LIVING WITH HIV
013.

AFRICAN AM AND DIABETES
010.

AFRICAN AM WOMEN: BREAST SCREEN BY
024.

AFRICAN AM; ASTHMA EDUCATION PROGRAM
017.

AFRICAN AMERICAN ADULTS; INJ DRUG USE
191.

AFRICAN AMERICAN DRUG USERS
183.

AFRICAN AMERICAN ELDERLY: HARLEM
174.

AFRICAN AMERICAN FAMILIES
185.

AFRICAN AMERICAN FAMILIES
172.

AFRICAN AMERICAN FEMALE BASKETBALL P
186.

AFRICAN AMERICAN MEN: PROSTATE SCREEN-
182.

AFRICAN AMERICAN MEN: PROSTATE CANCER
179.

AFRICAN AMERICAN MOTHERS; HAIR COMB-
184.

AFRICAN AMERICAN SMOKERS
197.

AFRICAN AMERICAN; RAPID END TO RENAL DIS
196.

AFRICAN AMERICANS AND DRUG USE
191.

AFRICAN AMERICANS AND ELECTIONS
199.

AFRICAN AMERICANS AND HEALTH CARE
171.

AFRICAN AMERICANS AND HEALTH STAKE
199.

AFRICAN AMERICANS, OLDER: & DIABETES
031.

AFRICAN AMERICANS WITH DISABILITIES
062.

AFRICAN AMERICANS: CANCER FATALISM
025.

AFRICAN AMERICANS: CANCER STATISTICS
026.

AFRICAN AMERICANS: INFANT MORTALITY
072.

AFRICAN AMERICANS: WAIT LONG FOR KIDNEY
041.

AFRICAN AMERICANS; ALCOHOL AND BLOOD P-
165.

AFRICAN AMERICANS; BEHAVIOR OF
003.

AFRICAN MEN IN LONDON: SEX BEHAVIOR
173.

AFRICAN MEN: EARLY DETECTION, PROSTATE
180.

AFRICAN-AM ADOLESCENTS IN HIGH-RISK ENV
011.

AFRICAN-AM ATTITUDES TO PROSTATE SCREEN
020.

AFRICAN-AM REPRESENTATION; NCI TRIALS
126.

AFRICAN-AM WOMEN IN PSYCHOTHERAPY
012.

AFRICAN-AMERICANS AND ANDROGENS
130.

AFRICAN-AMERICANS AND HLA-DQ3
069.

AFRO AMERICANS: ALLOCATION OF KIDNEYS
016.

AGE AND HIP FRACTURE
065.

AGE AND RELATIONS, DEMENTIA
123.

AGE AS MEDIATOR OF ANGER IN SUICIDE ATT-
188.

AGE AT ONSET OF VARICELLA
116.

AGE, WOMEN AND AIDS
159.

AGING PROJECT IN HARLEM: RESULTS OF
174.

AIDS AND SOUTH AFRICAN STUDENTS
125.

AIDS COUNSELING CENTERS
095.

AIDS PREVENTION IN HIGH-RISK WOMEN
014.

AIDS RISK, PERCEPTION OF
097.

AIDS: WHAT AFR-AM WOMEN DO & FEEL ABOUT
159.

AIDS-HIV WOMEN: SOCIO-DEMOGRAPHICS
177.

AIR POLLUTION EFFECT ON MINORITY POPUL
044.

ALCOHOL AND FEMALE BASKETBALL PLAYERS
186.

ALCOHOL CONSUMPTION
165.

ALCOHOL DURING PREGNANCY; WARNING
064.

ALCOHOL SURVEY, NATIONAL
189.

ALCOHOL USE AND PROSTATE CANCER RISK
015.

ALCOHOL: DRIVING UNDER THE INFLUENCE
189.

ALCOHOLIC BEVERAGES WARNING:HEEDING
064.

ALCOHOLICS AT A PSYCHIATRIC HOSPITAL
119.

ALCOHOLICS: ADULT CHILDREN OF
071.

ALCOHOLICS: ADULT CHILDREN OF
018.

ALLOCATION OF KIDNEYS TO AFR0-AM
016.

AMERICAN MINORITY GROUPS: EATING DISTRUB
042.

AN EXAM OF FEMALE BASKETBALL PLAYERS
186.

ANALYSIS, MUTATION
088.

ANDROGENS AND LIFE-STYLE FACTORS
130.

ANGER, MEDIATORS OF: SUICIDE ATTEMPTERS
188.

ANGLO WORKERS, GENDER & DISABILITY
038.

ANNUAL PROSTATE SCREEN: INTENTION
054.

ANTHROPOLOGY 'S HOODOO MUSEUM
019.

ANTIBIOTICS: BELIEF, USE N LOW ECON FAM
076.

APPENDICITIS AMONG BLACK SOUTH AFR
007.

APPLICATION OF SURROGATE LAWS
139.

ARTHROPLASTY, HIP
153.

ARTHROPLASTY, JOINT, TOTAL
153.

ASIAN, LATINO AND BLACK SEGREGATION
077.

ASIAN MEN AND ANDROGENS
130.

ASSOCIATION OF RACE / ETHNICITY: MAMMO-G
198.

ASSOCIATION OF SCHOOL-DROP-OUTS
191.

ASSOCIATIONS WITH MATERNAL HEALTH, BIR
006.

ASTHMA EDUCATION PROGRAM
017.

ASTHMA, RISKS FOR
101.

ATHEROSCLEROSIS RISK & COMM STUDY
079.

ATHEROSCLEROSIS RISK IN COMMUNITIES
168.

ATLANTIC CLINICS: BREAST CANCER & MAMM
128.

ATTACHMENT, LABOR FORCE
111.

ATTAINMENT, COMPENSATION & MENTORING
112.

ATTITUDES & PERCEPTIONS
098.

ATTITUDES, ABNORMAL EATING
005.

ATTITUDES OF AFRICAN-AM TO PROSTATE SCR
020.

ATTITUDES, RACIAL
049.

ATTITUDES TO RECTAL PROSTATE EXAM
037.

AUTOPSY-BASED STUDY: DISEASE TRENDS
091.

AUTOWORKERS' VULNERABILITY: UNEMPLOY
113.

AYANIAN JZ ET AL
192.

BACHMAN R ET AL
100.

BARNETT E ET AL
194.

BARRIERS, SOCIETAL; IN PSYCHOTHERAPY
012.

BARRIERS TO MEDICAL CARE
062.

BASKETBALL PLAYERS, FEMALE
186.

BEDER J
096.

BEHAVIOR, SEXUAL
173.

BEHAVIORAL ISSUES: WOMEN: HIV RISK
014.

BEHAVIORS, DRUG; FEMALE
186.

BEHAVIORS, HIGH RISK AND PERCEPTIONS
097.

BEHAVIORS OF AFRICAN AMERICANS
003.

BEHAVIORS: ABNORMAL EATING ATTITUDES
005.

BELIEF AND USE OF MEDICATIONS
076.

BELIEFS: CHILD REARING
027.

BERGMAN S ET AL
074.

BEVERAGES, ALCOHOLIC
064.

BIRD ST
129.

BIRTH WEIGHT, INFANT
006.

BIRTH WEIGHT INFANTS
121.

BLACK, ASIAN AND LATINO SEGREGATION
077.

BLACK ASTHMATIC CHILDREN
028.

BLACK IDENTITY AND DRINKING IN THE U.S.
021.

BLACK INFANT MORTALITY; TRENDS, U.S.
154.

BLACK KIDNEY DONORS: FEWER
056.

BLACK MALES: YOUNG AND TRAUMA
160.

BLACK MEN AND HEART DISEASE
194.

BLACK MEN AND WOMEN: DISADVANTAGED
002.

BLACK OLDER WORKERS
038.

BLACK POPULATION, RURAL AND CARCINOMA
035.

BLACK SOUTH AFRICANS: APPENDICITIS
007.

BLACK SUICIDE ATTEMPTERS
188.

BLACK WOMEN & LESS MAMMOGRAPHY
022.

BLACK WOMEN AND BREAST CANCER
023.

BLACK WOMEN AND MORE RISK IN CHD
176.

BLACK WOMEN, DEPRESSION
034.

BLACK WOMEN: MEASURE OF PHYSICAL ACTIV
083.

BLACK WOMEN: POLITICAL PARTICIPATION
082.

BLACKS: ADVERSE BYPASS SURGERY
008.

BLOOD PRESSURE; ALCOHOL, CHANGES IN
165.

BODY DISABILITY AND WALKING EFFECT
144.

BODY TYPE PREFERENCES
115.

BOUND J ET AL
111.

BOWER BL ET AL
186.

BOYD NR ET AL
197.

BRANSON BM ET AL
068.

BRAWLEY OW ET AL
161.

BREAST CANCER AND BLACK WOMEN
023.

BREAST CANCER AT TWO ATLANTIC CLINICS
128.

BREAST CANCER SCREENING
198.

BREAST CANCER; HOW RACE COLORS
092.

BREAST SCREENING
024.

BRODY GH ET AL
172.

BRODY GH ET AL
185.

BROMAN CL ET AL
113.

BROOKS-GUNN J ET AL
047.

BRYAN CF ET AL
016.

BURDEN OF SMOKING AND MORTALITY
140.

BURNS PB ET AL
136.

BURNS RB ET AL
022.

BURTON L ET AL
152.

BYPASS SURGERY: ADVERSE OUTCOME
008.

CAETANO R ET AL
189.

CALLAHAN CM ET AL
123.

CALLENDER CO ET AL
170.

CANADA: ANDROGENS AND LIFE-STYLE FACT
130.

CANCER, BREAST
023.

CANCER, BREAST
092.

CANCER, COLORECTAL; SURGERY FOR
137.

CANCER DETECTION: EDUCATING ABOUT
043.

CANCER FATALISM AMONG AFR-AM
025.

CANCER INFORMATION: AA SMOKERS
197.

CANCER OUTCOMES: AFRICAN-A, CAUCASIANS
162.

CANCER PREVENTION: EDUCATING A-AM
043.

CANCER, PROSTATE
015.

CANCER, PROSTATE: AFRICAN AMERICAN MEN
179.

CANCER, PROSTATE; AND RECTAL EXAM
037.

CANCER RISK: U.S. BLACKS AND WHITES
015.

CANCER SCREENING, BREAST
198.

CANCER SCREENING FOR PROSTATE
182.

CANCER STATISTICS FOR AFRICAN AMERICANS
026.

CANCER SURVIVAL: RACIAL GAPS IN
163.

CANCER: I HOPE i DON'T HAVE
001.

CARCINOMA, ORAL
035.

CARDIOVASCULAR DISEASE
167.

CARE, FOSTER, AND ABANDONMENT
169.

CARE, HEALTH: ATTITUDES OF WORKERS
049.

CARE; STRUCTURE OF INFORMAL
152.

CARIBBEAN MEN: SEXUAL BEHAVIOR
173.

CARIES, DENTAL
102.

CARTER JH
107.

CASE REPORTS: RELEVANCE OF RACE, ETHN
124.

CAUCASIANS AND AA: INFANT MORTALITY
072.

CHARACTERISTICS, WOMEN WITH HIV-AIDS
177.

CHD MORTALITY, RACIAL DISPARITIES
168.

CHEMOTHERAPY FOR PARASITE INFESTATIONS
138.

CHILD ADJUSTMENT
172.

CHILD COMPETENCE
185.

CHILD REARING BELIEFS
027.

CHILDHOOD SEXUAL ABUSE; EFFECTS OF
145.

CHILDHOOD SLEEP PROBLEMS
029.

CHILDREN, ADULT, OF ALCOHOLICS
018.

CHILDREN AND PARASITE INFESTATIONS
138.

CHILDREN, BLACK ASTHMATIC
028.

CHILDREN DAY CARE AND USE OF MATERIAL
155.

CHILDREN, PERI- AND PRE-NATAL; ASTHMA
101.

CHILDREN: ENVIRONMENTAL HEALTH THREATS
142.

CHILDREN: PASSIVE SMOKING IN
093.

CHILDREN'S INTELLIGENCE TEST SCORES
047.

CHISHOLM JF
085.

CHRONOLOGY OF SUCCESSES; HEALTH CARE
063.

CIGARETTE SMOKING
110.

CIGARETTE SMOKING AND CANCER RISK
136.

CIGARETTE SMOKING: ETHNIC DIFFERENCES
178.

CLARK DO
144.

CLARK DO ET AL
099.

CLASS ANALYSES: COGNITIVE IMPAIRMENT
174.

CLASS CA ET AL
104.

CLIENTS AND HIV ILLNESS
105.

CLINICAL CHARACTERISTICS: ASTHMATIC CHIL
028.

CLINICAL OUTCOMES, ENDOMETRIAL CANCER
164.

CLINICAL PRESENTATION: ALCOHOLICS
119.

CLINICAL SAMPLE OF DISADVANTAGED
002.

CO-SLEEPING AND SLEEP PROBLEMS
029.

COCAINE ABUSE
106.

COCAINE ADDICTION: TREATMENT
051.

COGNITIVE IMPAIRMENT
174.

COGNITIVE MEDIATORS: PRESCHOOL
030.

COLE ER ET AL
082.

COLLEGIATE ADULT CHILDREN OF ALCOHOLICS
018.

COLLINS JW JR ET AL
121.

COLON CANCER: OUTCOMES IN
162.

COLOR, PEOPLE OF: TREATMENT
061.

COLORECTAL CANCER; SURGERY FOR
137.

COLPOSCOPY AND MINORITY WOMEN
001.

COMBAT VETERANS AND PTSD
118.

COMBING, HAIR: INTERACTIONS
184.

COMMUNICATION CAMPAIGN: CANCER INFO
197.

COMMUNITY AND DRUG USE
055.

COMMUNITY: PRETERM BIRTH IN THE
103.

COMMUNITY; HEALTH CARE IN THE
063.

COMMUNITY; REACHING OUT
120.

COMPLICATIONS, PREGNANCY; & HYPERTEN
081.

CONDOM USE, PREDICTORS
011.

CONDOMS
011.

CONFLICTING STEREOTYPES
187.

CONSUMPTION, ALCOHOL
165.

CONTRACEPTIVE PRACTICES
132.

CONTROL, TOBACCO
088.

COOPER GS ET AL
137.

COPING DIABETES
031.

COPING QUESTIONNAIRE
053.

COPING WITH COST OF DRUGS
032.

COPING; VIOLENCE AND
122.

CORNELIUS JR ET AL
119.

CORNELIUS LJ ET AL
062.

CORNELL PP ET AL
164.

CORONARY ARTERY BYPASS; ADVERSE
008.

CORONARY HEART DISEASE, INCREASING
194.

CORONARY HEART DISEASE: WOMEN RISK
176.

COST OF DRUGS; COPING WITH THE
032.

COTININE, EXPOSURE TO
093.

CRAGO M ET AL
042.

CRISIS: HIV-AIDS SYNDROME
195.

CUFFE SP ET AL
108.

CULTURAL FACTORS: HYPERTENSION
070.

CUTIS A ET AL
165.

DANCH B
159.

DANIGELLIS NL ET AL
024.

DANSKY BS ET AL
156.

DAWSON G
009.

DEBATE, ADOPTION
057.

DEGAZON CD
031.

DEMENTIA AND RELATIONSHIPS
123.

DENNIS GC
195.

DENTAL CARIES
102.

DENTAL EDUCATION: DISCRIMINATION
039.

DEPRESSION IN BLACK & WHITE WOMEN
034.

DEPRIVATION, ECONOMIC
047.

DETECTION, CANCER
043.

DETECTION, EARLY: PROSTATE CANCER
180.

DETECTION OF HPOV DNA
035.

DI CLEMENTE RJ ET AL
011.

DIABETES
010.

DIABETES, COPING
031.

DIABETES IN URBAN AFRICAN-AM
036.

DIABETES, TYPE II
033.

DIABETIC END STAGE RENAL DISEASE: SURVIV
087.

DIABETIC TYPE
087.

DIETARY FACTORS; ROLE IN HYPERTENSION
127.

DIFFERENCES IN BODY TYPE PREFERENCES
115.

DIFFERENCES IN HOME OWNERSHIP
117.

DIFFERENCES, PSYCHOLOGICAL : VETERANS
118.

DIFFERENCES, RACIAL: HERPES, VARICELLA
116.

DIFFERENCES, RACIAL: RENAL TRANSPLANT-
192.

DIFFERENCES: COLORECTAL CANCER; RACE
137.

DIFFERENTIALS, SOCIO-ECONOMIC
135.

DIGITAL RECTAL EXAMINATIONS
037.

DIGNAM JJ ET AL
162.

DISABILITIES AND BARRIERS TO MED CARE
062.

DISABILITY STATUS
038.

DISABILITY STATUS AND RACE DIFFERENCES
111.

DISADVANTAGED AND MASTECTOMY
096.

DISADVANTAGED FAMILIES: WELL BEING
075.

DISADVANTAGED MEN AND WOMEN
002.

DISCRIMINATION IN DENTAL EDUCATION
039.

DISEASE, CARDIOVASCULAR
167.

DISEASE, GRAVES'
069.

DISEASE, KIDNEY
074.

DISEASE, RENAL
074.

DISEASE TRENDS, OCCUPATIONAL
091.

DISORDERS, PSYCHIATRIC
104.

DISTURBANCES, EATING
042.

DIVERSITY IN MEDICINE
40.

DNA, PAPILLOMAVIRUS; DETECTION OF
035.

DOCTORS' ADVISE: SMOKING
094.

DOMESTIC VIOLENCE: POLICE INVOLVEMENT
100.

DONATION PROBLEM: ORGAN-TISSUE
170.

DONATION: SOLUTION
170.

DONORS, KIDNEY; FEWER
056.

DREHER GF ET AL
112.

DRESSLER WW
070.

DRINKING AND BLACK IDENTITY
021.

DRIVING UNDER THE INFLUENCE OF ALCOHOL
189.

DROP-OUTS, SCHOOL
191.

DRUG ABUSE AND VOCATIONAL CAREER
141.

DRUG BEHAVIORS: FEMALE BASKETBALL P-
186.

DRUG USE AND VOCATIONAL CAREER
141.

DRUG USE, INJECTING
191.

DRUG USE: PREDICTING CHANGE IN
055.

DRUG USERS, AFRICAN AMERICAN
183.

DRUGS, PRESCRIPTION
032.

DRUGS, THE COST OF
032.

DUMMETT CO
039.

DWORKN RH
116.

EATING ATTITUDES, ABNORMAL
005.

EATING DISORDER SYMPTOMS
131.

EATING DISTURBANCES: MINORITY GROUPS
042.

ECONOMIC DEPRIVATION
047.

ECONOMICALLY DISADVANTAGED FAM
075.

ECONOMICS AND SUBSTANCE USE
193.

EDITORIAL: AFFIRMATIVE ACTION POLITICS
009.

EDITORIAL: DIVERSITY IN MEDICINE
040.

EDITORIAL: PERCEPTIONS, AF-AM PHYSICIANS
149.

EDUCATING AFRICAN AMERICANS: CANCER
043.

EDUCATION AND DEMENTIA
123.

EDUCATION PROGRAM: ASTHMA
017.

EDUCATION, WOMEN AND AIDS
159.

EDUCATIONAL RESOURCE MATERIALS; USE
155.

EDUCATIONAL VARIABLES
098.

EDWARDS D
078.

EFFECTIVENESS TRIAL: OF AIDS
004.

ELDERLY IN CENTRAL HARLEM
174.

ELDERLY, US: FRACTURES
065.

ELECTIONS AND AFRICAN AMERICANS
199.

ELLIS GA ET AL
088.

EMONT SL ET AL
140.

EMOTIONAL CONCERNS OF TOWNSHIP YOUTH
157.

EMPLOYMENT, MEDICAL CARE
084.

END STAGE RENAL DISEASE
074.

END STAGE RENAL DISEASE
087.

ENDOMETRIAL CARCINOMA
164.

ENVIRONMENT, HOME
047.

ENVIRONMENTAL HEALTH THREATS: CHIL
142.

ENVIRONMENTS, HIGH RISK
011.

EPIDEMIC, HIV
051.

EPIDEMIOLOGY OF HYPERTENSION
046.

EPIDEMIOLOGY OF PROSTATE NEOPLASM
045.

EQUITY, HOME
117.

ESPARZA DV ET AL
145.

ESTABLISHMENT OF MENTORING REL
112.

ESTIMATION OF COGNITIVE IMPAIRMENT
174.

ETHNIC DIFFERENCES: CHIL INTELL
047.

ETHNIC DIFFERENCES: CIGARETTE SMOKING
178.

ETHNIC GROUP RELEVANCE IN CASE REPORTS
124.

ETHNIC GROUPS
048.

ETHNIC GROUPS & EATING ATTITUDES
005.

ETHNICALLY SENSITIVE MESSENGERS
049.

ETHNICITY AND PSYCHOTHERAPY
050.

ETHNICITY EFFECTS: SLEEP
029.

EVANS BA ET AL
173.

EVIDENCE, INCREASING: HEART DISEASE MORT-
194.

EVIDENCE OF GROWTH: HIV EPIDEMIC
051.

EXAMINATION OF RACIAL DIFFERENCES: CVD
167.

EXAMINATION OF REALITIES; HEALTH CARE
063.

EXAMINATIONS, DIGITAL, RECTAL
037.

EXPERIENCES OF LOW INCOME YOUTH
066.

EXPLORATION OF RACIAL ATTITUDES
049.

EXPLORATORY STUDY: CHIL OF ALCOHOLICS
018.

EXPLORING PURPOSE: PRENATAL CARE SERV
052.

EXPOSURE TO COTININE
093.

EXPOSURES, MULTIPLE, TO VIOLENCE
122.

FAMILIES; SUPPORT, WELL BEING IN DISADV
075.

FAMILY PROCESSES
172.

FAMILY-SUPPORT MEDIATORS: PRESCHOOL
030.

FANTUZZO JW ET AL
150.

FATALISM, CANCER
025.

FAULKNER DL ET AL
110.

FEE ABOUT AIDS: AFR-AM WOMEN
159.

FEE ABOUT AIDS: WHAT AFR-AM WOMEN
159.

FEMALE BASKETBALL PLAYERS
186.

FEMALE BRITISH POPULATION: EATING ATTITUD
005.

FEMORAL NECK FRACTURES
065.

FENSTER A
061.

FERGUSON JA ET AL
167.

FERTILITY TIMING
175.

FILARDO EK
060.

FILLENBAUM GG ET AL
055.

FIRST DEGREE RELATIVES: KIDNEY DISEASE
074.

FLEXNER REPORT
086.

FORCE FIELD ANALYSIS
088.

FORD DY ET AL
098.

FORD ME ET AL
017.

FORENSIC IMPLICATIONS: ADOPTION DEBATE
057.

FOSTER CARE AND POLITICS OF ABANDON-M
169.

FOULKS EF ET AL
050.

FOX K
019.

FRACTURE, HIP
065.

FRACTURES, TROCHANTERIC
065.

FREY WH ET AL
077.

FRIEDMAN AS ET AL
057.

FRIEDMAN AS ET AL
141.

FRUEH BC ET AL
118.

FULTON J ET AL
007.

FUNCTIONING, MATERNAL PSYCHOLOGICAL
172.

GAMBLE VN: 47 REFERENCES
171.

GAPS, RACIAL, IN CANCER SURVIVAL
163.

GAZMARARIAN JA ET AL
034.

GELFAND DE ET AL
037.

GENDER AND COMPENSATION AND MENTOR
112.

GENDER AND RACE DIFFERENCES
108.

GENDER AND RESPONSE TO STRESS
113.

GENDER DIFFERENCES, CVD MANAGEMENT
167.

GENDER DIFFERENCES: EARLY LIFE RISK
057.

GENDER DIFFERENCES: HOSPITALIZED ADULTS
166.

GENDER DIFFERENCES: OUTCOME QUESTION
058.

GENDER ISSUES: WOMEN: HIV RISK
014.

GENDER ON LABOR SUPPLY
038.

GENDER PATTERNS: SOCIAL INTERACTIONS
060.

GENDER, RACE DIFFERENCES: HOSPITAL
166.

GENDER: VICTIMIZATION AND PTSD
156.

GENE, TSC2
088.

GENERATIONAL RELATIONSHIPS: BIRTHS
147.

GEOGRAPHIC PATTERNS: FRACTURES
065.

GERHARD GT ET AL
176.

GERONIMUS AT ET AL
175.

GHANAIAN IMMIGRANTS
033.

GILLUM RF
046.

GIRLS: WEIGHT MODIFICATION EFFORTS
158.

GLOBULINS, SEX HORMONE BINDING
130.

GLUCOSE DISPOSAL RATES
033.

GLUCOSE INTOLERANCE
033.

GODBOLD DT ET AL
160.

GOLD MINERS
091.

GRAVES' DISEASE
069.

GRAY RJ ET AL
008.

GREENBERG DR ET AL
115.

GREENE B
012.

GREENLAND S ET AL
051.

GRIESLER PC ET AL
178.

GRIFFIN LW ET AL
056.

GRIFFITH EE
057.

GRISSO JA ET AL
073.

GROUP THERAPY
061.

GROWTH OF HIV EPIDEMIC
051.

HAIR COMBING INTERACTIONS
184.

HAIR, COTININE IN
093.

HANKIN JR ET AL
064.

HARLEM AND ELDERLY AFRICAN AMERICANS
174.

HARLEM RESULTS: AGING ELDERLY
174.

HARRIS DR ET AL
166.

HARRIS RM ET AL
097.

HASBROUCK LM
086.

HAYES RB ET AL
015.

HAYLEY DC ET AL
139.

HAYWARD MD ET AL
114.

HEALTH CARE FOR UNDER-SERVED POPUL
151.

HEALTH CARE IN THE AFRICAN-AM COMMUNITY
063.

HEALTH CARE SURROGATE LAWS
139.

HEALTH CARE WORKERS & ATTITUDES
049.

HEALTH CARE: AFRICAN AMERICANS
171.

HEALTH CARE; MILLION VOICES FOR
003.

HEALTH INEQUALITY
175.

HEALTH, MATERNAL
006.

HEALTH, MENTAL: ISSUES
085.

HEALTH OF AFRICAN AMERICANS
199.

HEALTH, PERCEIVED
095.

HEALTH RESEARCH, MINORITY
161.

HEALTH SECTOR JOBS
084.

HEALTH STUDY: PRE-ADOLES GIRLS
158.

HEALTH THREATS, ENVIRONMENTAL: CHIL
142.

HEALTH VALUES
003.

HEALTH-WEALTH CONNECTION
146.

HEART DISEASE AND LOWER SOCIAL CLASS
194.

HEEDING ALCOHOLIC BEVERAGE WARNING
064.

HELP-SEEKING BY AFRICAN AM: DRUG USERS
183.

HEMODIALYSIS
087.

HEMODIALYSIS PATIENTS
190.

HERD D ET AL
021.

HERPES ZOSTER
116.

HETEROGENEITY OF HIP FRACTURE
065.

HETEROSEXUAL EXPERIENCES: YOUTH
066.

HETHERINGTON SE ET AL
014.

HIGH RISK ENVIRONMENTS
011.

HIGH RISK WOMEN: AIDS PREVENTION
014.

HILL HM ET AL
122.

HIMMELSTEIN DU ET AL
084.

HIP ARTHROPLASTY
153.

HIP FRACTURE
065.

HISPANIC AMERICANS WITH DISABILITIES
062.

HISPANIC YOUTH
066.

HISPANICS AND NIC TRIALS
126.

HISTORY, OFFENDERS'
100.

HISTORY, SEXUAL ASSAULT
131.

HIV EPIDEMIC; GROWTH OF
051.

HIV ILLNESS
095.

HIV ILLNESS; PSYCHOSOCIAL OUTCOMES
105.

HIV SEXUAL RISK REDUCTION INTERVENTION
068.

HIV SEXUAL RISK-REDUCTION INTERVENTION
067.

HIV, STD AND PREGNANCY PREVENTION
132.

HIV: WOMEN LIVING WITH
013.

HIV-AIDS WOMEN
177.

HLA CLASS I ANTIBODY
041.

HLA-DQ3
069.

HOFFMAN JA ET AL
106.

HOGUE CJ ET AL
103.

HOME ENVIRONMENT
047.

HOME EQUITY
117.

HOME OWNERSHIP
117.

HOOD RG
199.

HOODOO MUSEUM
019.

HOPE FOR REMEDIES
063.

HORMONE BINDING, SEX
130

HOSPITAL SETTING AND DIABETES
036.

HOWARD DL ET AL
143.

HYBRIDIZATION, IN SITU
035.

HYMOWITZ N ET AL
094.

HYPERTENSION
070.

HYPERTENSION AND ROLE OF DIETARY FAC
127.

HYPERTENSION, MATERNAL
081.

HYPERTENSION: EPIDEMIOLOGY OF
046.

HYPERTENSION; LIFE EVENTS AND
077.

HYPERTENSIVE AFRICAN AMERICANS
196.

HYPERTENSIVE END STAGE RENAL DIS
074.

IDENTITIES; WOMEN IN PSYCHOTHERAPY
012.

IDENTITY, BLACK, AND DRINKING
021.

IDENTITY, POLITICAL
082.

ILLNESS, HIV
105.

ILLNESS, HIV
095.

IMMIGRANTS, GHANAIAN
033.

IMPACT OF ENVIRONMENT HEALTH THREATS
142.

IN SITU HYBRIDIZATION
035.

INCIDENCE AND RACE: SMOKING
110.

INDIANA, SMOKING AND MORTALITY
140.

INEQUALITY, HEALTH
175.

INEQUITIES IN MEN'S RETIREMENT
114.

INFANT BIRTH WEIGHT
006.

INFANT MORTALITY
072.

INFANT MORTALITY AND BIRTHWEIGHTS
147.

INFANT MORTALITY MODELS
129.

INFANT MORTALITY; TRENDS; U.S.
154.

INFANTS, NON-LOW BIRTH WEIGHT
121.

INFECTION, SEXUALLY TRANSMITTED
173.

INFESTATIONS, PARASITE
138.

INFORMAL CARE
152.

INFORMATION, CANCER, FOR AS SMOKERS
197.

INJECTING DRUG USE
191.

INJURIES AMONG MINORITY WOMEN
073.

INJURY, VICTIM
100.

INNER CITY WOMEN: INJURIES
073.

INNOVATIVE STRATEGIES: REACHING OUT
120.

INSULIN MEDIATED GLUCOSE DISPOSAL RATES
033.

INTELLIGENCE AS MEDIATOR OF ANGER
188.

INTELLIGENCE SCORES
047.

INTENTION TO UNDERGO PROSTATE SCREEN
054.

INTERVENTION, HIV RISK
067.

ISSUES IN AIDS PREVENTION
014.

ISSUES IN MEDICINE AND PSY
107.

JOBS, HEALTH SECTOR
084.

JOINT ARTHROPLASTY, TOTAL
153.

KANDAKAI TL ET AL
076.

KARAGAS MR ET AL
065.

KIDNEY
041.

KIDNEY DISEASE; 1ST DEGREE RELATIVES
074.

KIDNEY DONORS, FEWER
056.

KIDNEYS, ALLOCATION
016.

KINSHIP SUPPORT
075.

KNIGHT JM ET AL
093.

KNOW ABOUT AIDS: WHAT AFR-AM WOMEN
159.

KNOWLEDGE OF MEDICATIONS IN LOW ECON
076.

KNOWLEDGE, REL, AIDS, SEX; STUDENTS
125.

KOMAROMY M ET AL
151.

KORENSTEIN K ET AL
102.

KUMAR A ET AL
089.

KUSHNER RF ET AL
083.

KUSKA B
163.

LABEL, WARNING; ALCOHOLIC
064.

LABOR FORCE, RACE DIFFERENCES
111.

LABOR SUPPLY
038.

LATINO, ASIAN, BLACK SEGREGATION
077.

LATINO OLDER WORKERS
038.

LAVIZZO-MOUREY R ET AL
149.

LAWS A ET AL
131.

LAWS, SURROGATE
139.

**LESTER D
072.**

**LESTER D
188.**

**LEWIS ML
184.**

**LIDDELL C
155.**

**LIFE EVENTS AN HYPERTENSION
077.**

**LIFE RISK, EARLY
057.**

**LIFE-STYLE FACTORS AND ANDROGENS
130.**

**LINN JG ET AL
105.**

**LINN JG ET AL
095.**

**LITERATURE: CHILDREN OF ALCOHOLICS
071.**

**LIVING WITH HIV: WOMEN
013.**

**LONDON, MEN AND SEXUAL BEHAVIOR
173.**

LONGSHORE D
183.

LOS ANGELES COUNTY AND HIV
051.

LOS ANGELES: HIV AND AIDS WOMEN
177.

LOW INCOME COMMUNITY; MOBILIZING
088.

LOW INCOME YOUTH
066.

LOW INCOME YOUTHS AND AIDS
004.

LOWE JI ET AL
043.

LOWE NK
181.

LOZOFF B ET AL
029.

LUGER AM ET AL
041.

LUYT DK ET AL
028.

MALE COHORTS AND HIV EPIDEMIC
051.

MALE SAMPLE: DRUG -USE-ABUSE
141.

MALES: YOUNG AND TRAUMA
160.

MAMMOGRAPHY
022.

MAMMOGRAPHY
198.

MAMMOGRAPHY AT TWO ATLANTIC CLINICS
128.

MAMMOGRAPHY USE
080.

MANAGEMENT OF CARDIOVASCULAR DISEASE
167.

MANAGEMENT OF TYPE II DIABETES
036.

MARRIAGE; ROLE OF
034.

MASTECTOMY
096.

MATCH AND SURROGATE LAWS
139.

MATERIALS, RESOURCE
155.

MATERNAL CHARACTERISTICS & CHL INTELL
047.

MATERNAL DEVELOPMENTAL GOALS
185.

MATERNAL EFFICACY BELIEFS
185.

MATERNAL HEALTH
006.

MATERNAL HYPERTENSION
081.

MATERNAL PSYCHOLOGICAL FUNCTIONING
172.

MATERNAL RACE AND PRETERM RISK
121.

MATERNAL WELL-BEING IN DISADVANT FAM
075.

MC FARLANE J ET AL
006.

MEASUREMENT MODEL: MEDICAL OUTCOMES
002.

MEASUREMENT OF PHYSICAL ACTIVITY
083.

MEASURES OF COMBAT VETS FOR PTSD
118.

MEDIATORS OF ANGER
188.

MEDIATORS OF PRESCHOOL EFFECTIVENESS
030.

MEDICAL CARE EMPLOYMENT IN U.S.
084.

MEDICAL CARE; BARRIERS TO
062.

MEDICAL OUTCOMES STUDY
002.

MEDICARE
137.

MEDICATIONS: BELIEFS, USE
076.

MEDICINE, DIVERSITY IN
040.

MEDICINE; ISSUES IN
107.

MEDINA RA ET AL
087.

MEN, AFRICAN: SEXUAL BEHAVIOR
173.

MEN AND ANDROGENS: US & CANADA
130.

MEN AND HIV EPIDEMIC
051.

MEN AND WOMEN
002.

MEN AND WOMEN: SEX ASSAULT HISTORY, ET
131.

MEN AND WOMEN; RETIREMENT
099.

MEN, BLACK: HEART DISEASE
104.

MEN: ATTITUDES TO RECTAL PROSTATE EXAM
037.

MEN: BODY TYPE PREFERENCES
115.

MEN: SEXUAL BEHAVIOR
173.

MEN: STOMACH CANCER RISK
136.

MEN'S RETIREMENT
114.

MENTAL DISTRESS
095.

MENTAL HEALTH ISSUES
085.

MENTORING RELATIONSHIPS
112.

MESSENGERS, SENSITIVE
049.

METABOLIC SYNDROME
079.

METHADONE DEPENDENT WOMEN
097.

MILLAR J ET AL
048.

MILLER DK ET AL
090.

MINERS, GOLD
091.

MINORITIES IN MEDICINE
086.

MINORITY ADVANTAGE IN DIABETIC RENAL DIS
087.

MINORITY GROUPS: EATING DISTURBANCES
042.

MINORITY HEALTH RESEARCH
151.

MINORITY MOTHERS AND SEX ABUSE
145.

MINORITY POPULATIONS & AIR POLLUTION
044.

MINORITY WOMEN
001.

MINORITY WOMEN: INJURIES
073.

MITCHELL AA ET AL
049.

MODELS, INFANT MORTALITY
129.

MOKOENA TR ET AL
133.

MOORMEIER J
023.

MORTALITY, CHD
168.

MORTALITY, INFANT
072.

MORTALITY MODELS; INFANT
129.

MORTALITY RISK
135.

MORTALITY RISK OF SCREENED MEN
135.

MOSBY JA
124.

MOTHER BIRTHWEIGHT & INFANT BIRTH WT
147.

MOTHERHOOD, USA: SAFE
181.

MOTHERS, ADOLESCENT; CHIL SEX ABUSE
145.

MOTHERS, BIRTHWEIGHTS & INFANT B-W
147.

MOTHERS, VIOLENCE & COPING STRATEGIES
122.

MOTT L
142.

MULTI-ETHNIC METROS AND SEGREGATION
077.

MULTI-PARAE AND ALCOHOL
064.

MULTIPLE RISK FACTOR INTERVENTION TRIAL
135.

MURDOCH RO
193.

MURRAY J ET AL
091.

MUSEUM, HOODOO
019.

MUTANS STREPTOCOCCI
102.

MUTATION-ANALYSIS
089.

MYERS RE ET AL
054.

MYERS SL JR ET AL
117.

NATIONAL ALCOHOL SURVEY
189.

NCI TREATMENT TRIALS: REPRESENTATION
126.

NEBEKER RS ET AL
058.

NECK, FEMORAL: FRACTURES
065.

NEOPLASM, PROSTATIC
045.

NEW YORK CITY AND ABANDONMENT
169.

NORRIS AE ET AL
066.

NOVEMBER ELECTIONS AND AFRICAN AM-
199.

NULLIPARAE AND ALCOHOL
064.

NURSING HOME RESIDENTS: PSY DISORDERS
104.

NUTRITIONAL RISK: OLDER BLACK AM
090.

O'MALLEY MS ET AL
198.

OBESE WOMEN
083.

OBOT IS ET AL
191.

OCCUPATION AND DEMENTIA
123.

OCCUPATION AND STOMACH CANCER RISK
136.

OCCUPATIONAL DISEASE TRENDS
091.

OFFENDER'S HISTORY OF VIOLENCE
100.

OFOSU MH ET AL
069.

OLDEN K
044.

OLIVETI JF ET AL
101.

OPPORTUNITY: COMPENSATION & MENTORING
112.

ORAL CARCINOMA
035.

ORGAN PROCUREMENT
049.

OSEI K ET AL
033.

OUTCOME AND RACE: PTSD
109.

OUTCOME QUESTIONNAIRE; GENDER DIFF
058.

OUTCOMES IN COLON CANCER
162.

OUTCOMES, PSYCHOSOCIAL; HIV
105.

OUTCOMES, STUDY; MEDICAL
002.

OUTCOMES: COCAINE TREATMENT
106.

OUTREACH: HOW RACE COLORS BREAST CA
092.

PAPILLOMAVIRUS DNA
035.

PARASITE INFESTATIONS
138.

PARENT, SINGLE
172.

PARENT, SINGLE AA FAMILIES
185.

PARENTING PRACTICES
185.

PARKINSON'S DISEASE
174.

PARTNERSHIPS, LOW INCOME YOUTH
066.

PASSIVE SMOKING IN CHILDREN
093.

PAST QUIT SMOKING ASSISTANCE
094.

PATIENTS, AFRO-AM: ALLOCATION, KIDNEYS
016.

PATIENTS, HEMODIALYSIS
190.

PATIENTS' PREFERENCE: RENAL TRANSPL
192.

PEDIATRIC CARE
027.

PEOPLE OF COLOR; TREATMENT
061.

PERCEIVED COMPETENCE & SOCIAL ACCEPT
151.

PERCEPTION OF AIDS RISK
097.

PERCEPTIONS OF AF-AM PHYSICIANS
149.

PERCEPTIONS OF STUDENTS
098.

PERI-NATAL RISK FOR ASTHMA
101.

PHYSICAL ACTIVITY, MEASUREMENT
083.

PHYSICAL FUNCTION AMONG RETIRED
099.

PHYSICIANS, ROLE: UNDERSERVED POPUL]
151.

PICTORIAL SCALE
150.

POLEDNAK AP
154.

POLICE INVOLVEMENT: DOMESTIC VIOLENCE
100.

POLICY IMPLICATIONS: ADOPTION
057.

POLITICAL IDENTITY
082.

POLITICAL PARTICIPATION: B-W WOMEN
082.

POLITICS, AFFIRMATIVE ACTION
009.

POLITICS OF ABANDONMENT IN NEW YORK CITY
169.

POLLUTION, AIR
044.

POPULATION, FEMALE; EATING ATTITUDES
005.

POPULATION STUDY: MINORITY WOMEN INJUR
073.

POPULATION VARIATION IN FERTILITY TIMING
175.

POPULATIONS, UNDER-SERVED
151.

POWE BD
025.

POWELL I
179.

PRACTICES, CONTRACEPTIVE
132.

PRACTICES, PARENTING
185.

PREDICTING CHANGE IN DRUG USE
055.

PREDICTORS OF CONDOM USE
011.

PREFERENCES, BODY TYPE
115.

PREGNANCY, ABUSE DURING
006.

PREGNANCY AND ALCOHOLIC WARNING
064.

PREGNANCY AND HYPERTENSION
081.

PREGNANCY PREVENTION
132.

PREMENSTRUAL BLACK WOMEN AND RISK
176.

PRENATAL CARE
052.

PRENATAL RISK FOR ASTHMA
101.

PRESCHOOL EFFECTIVENESS
030.

PRESCRIPTION DRUGS AND COST
032.

PRESSURE, BLOOD, AND ALCOHOL
165.

PRETERM BIRTH IN AA COMMUNITY
103.

PRETERM RISK
121.

PRETERN INFANTS IN STILL-FACE SITUATION
134.

PREVALENCE OF COGNITIVE IMPAIRMENT
174.

PREVENTION, AIDS; WOMEN
014.

PREVENTION, CANCER
043.

PREVENTION, PREGNANCY
132.

PREVENTION PROGRAM, AIDS
004.

PROCESSES, FAMILY
172.

PROCUREMENT, ORGAN
049.

PROSTATE CANCER
015.

PROSTATE CANCER AND RECTAL EXAM
037.

PROSTATE CANCER: ADDRESS
179.

PROSTATE CANCER: EARLY DETECTION
180.

PROSTATE PREDICTOR FOR SCREENING
182.

PROSTATE SCREENING
020.

PROSTATE SCREENING INTENTION
054.

PROSTATIC NEOPLASM
045.

PROTEINURIA
196.

PSYCHIATRIC DISORDERS; NURSING RESIDENTS
104.

PSYCHIATRIC DISORDERS; TREATMENT DIFF
108.

PSYCHIATRIC HOSPITAL AND ALCOHOLICS
119.

PSYCHIATRY: ISSUES IN
107.

PSYCHOLOGICAL FACTORS: HYPERTENSION
070.

PSYCHOLOGICAL FUNCTIONING: MATERNAL
172.

PSYCHOLOGICAL ISSUES: WOMEN: HIV RISK
014.

PSYCHOLOGICAL MEASURES: DIFFER; VETS
118.

PSYCHOSOCIAL CULTURAL ISSUES: MED & P
107.

PSYCHOSOCIAL OUTCOMES; HIV
105.

PSYCHOSOCIAL TREATMENTS: COCAINE ABUS
106.

PSYCHOTHERAPY; ETHNICITY AND
050.

PSYCHOTHERAPY; WOMEN IN
012.

PTSD
118.

PTSD: VETERANS SUFFERING FROM
109.

PTSD; VICTIMIZATION AND
156.

PUBLIC HOUSING ADOLESCENTS & CONDOMS
011.

PURPOSE OF LIFE AND PRENATAL CARE
052.

QUALITY OF LIFE: HEMODIALYSIS PATIENTS
190.

QUESTIONNAIRE: WAYS OF COPING
053.

RACE AND GENDER DIFFERENCES
108.

RACE AND HIP FRACTURE
065.

RACE AND INCIDENCE: CIGARETTE SMOKING
110.

RACE AND MIXED GROUPS: SOCIAL INTERACT
060.

RACE AND OUTCOME OF PTSD
109.

RACE AND OUTCOMES
161.

RACE AND OUTCOMES IN ENDOMETRIAL CA
164.

RACE AND PRETERM RISK
121.

RACE AND RESPONSE TO STRESS
113.

RACE DIFFERENCES AND COLORECTAL CANCER
137.

RACE DIFFERENCES IN LABOR FORCE ATTACH
111.

RACE, DOMESTIC VIOLENCE
100.

RACE, HOW IT COLORS BREAST CANCER
092.

RACE INEQUITIES IN MEN'S RETIREMENT
114.

RACE RELEVANCE IN CASE REPORTS
124.

RACE: COMPENSATION AND MENTORING
112.

RACIAL ATTITUDES
049.

RACIAL DIFFERENCES
156.

RACIAL DIFFERENCES & BODY TYPE PREFER
115.

RACIAL DIFFERENCES: ACCESS TO TRANSPL
192.

RACIAL DIFFERENCES: CARDIOVAS DISEASE
167.

RACIAL DIFFERENCES: HERPES & VARICELLA
116.

RACIAL DIFFERENCES: HOME OWNERSHIP
117.

RACIAL DIFFERENCES: SMOKING
093.

RACIAL DIFFERENCES: VETERANS & PTSD
118.

RACIAL DIFFERENCES; HEALTH-WEALTH
146.

RACIAL DISPARITIES IN CHD MORTALITY
168.

RACIAL EFFECTS: ALCOHOLICS AT PSYCH H
119.

RACIAL GAPS IN CANCER SURVIVAL
163.

RACIAL, GENDER DIFFERENCES: HOSPITAL
166.

RANKIN EA ET AL
153.

RATIONALE FOR A-AM DIABETES
010.

RAYLOR M ET AL
138.

REACHING OUT TO COMMUNITY
120.

REALITIES: HEALTH CARE
063.

REARING, CHILD; BELIEF
027.

REASONS: DIABETES
010.

RECOMMENDATIONS FOR MAMMOGRAPHY
198.

RECTAL EXAMINATIONS
037.

REISS D
005.

RELATIONSHIPS, MENTORING
112.

RELATIVES, FIRST DEGREE
074.

RELEVANCE OF RACE OR ETHNIC GROUP
124.

RELIGIOSITY: SOUTH AFRICAN STUDENTS
125.

REMEDIES, HOPE FOR
063.

RENAL DISEASE
074.

RENAL DISEASE SURVIVAL ON HEMODIALYSIS
087.

RENAL DISEASE: RAPID PROGRESSION TO END
196.

RENAL TRANSPLANTATION
192.

REPRESENTATION IN NCI TREATMENT RIALS
126.

RESEARCH, MINORITY HEALTH
161,

RESEARCH, NEW: HAIR COMBING
184.

RESEARCH: A-M DIABETES
010.

RESIDENTIAL SEGREGATION
154.

RESIDENTS, NURSING HOME; PSY DISORD
104.

RESOURCE MATERIALS, ED; USE OF
155.

RESPONSE TO STRESS
113.

RESPONSIBILITY, SOCIAL
082.

RETIREMENT AGED; PHYSICAL FUNCTION
099.

RETIREMENT, MEN'S
114.

REVIEW, LITERATURE: CANCER PREV, DETEC
043.

REVIEW: CANCER FATALISM
025.

REVIEW: EATING DISTURBANCES
042.

REVIEW: ORGAN-TISSUE DONATION
170.

REYNOLDS AJ ET AL
030.

RISK, AIDS; PERCEPTION OF
097.

RISK, HIV SEXUAL
067.

RISK, NUTRITIONAL
090.

RISK, PRETERM
121.

RISK REDUCTION INTERVENTION; HIV
067.

RISK REDUCTION; WOMEN; HV
068.

RISK, STOMACH CANCER; MEN AND WOMEN
136.

ROBINSON KD ET AL
120.

ROBINSON SB ET AL
020.

RODNEY HE
071.

RODNEY HE ET AL
018.

ROLE OF DIETARY FACTORS IN HYPERTENSION
127.

ROLE OF MARRIAGE
034.

ROSENHECK R ET AL
109.

ROSENWALD FUND SYPHILIS STUDIES
148.

ROSNER D ET AL
169.

ROY B
148.

SAKR WA ET AL
045.

SAMADI AR ET AL
081.

SANDERSON M ET AL
147.

SANDRICK KM
092.

SANTIAGO AM ET AL
038.

SCALE, PICTORIAL
150.

SCHMIDT MI ET AL
079.

SCHOOL DROP-OUTS
191.

SCHOOL, STUDENTS PERCEPTIONS, ATTITUDE
098.

SCHREIBER GB ET AL
158.

SCORES, INTELLIGENCE
047.

SCREENING, BREAST
024.

SCREENING, BREAST CANCER
198.

SCREENING INTENTION, PROSTATE
054.

SCREENING, PROSTATE
182.

SCREENING, PROSTATE CANCER
020.

SEGAL LB ET AL
134.

SEGREGATION, RESIDENTIAL
154.

SENSITIVE MESSENGERS
049.

SEROPREVALENCE STUDIES
148.

SERUM ANDROGENS AND LIFE-STYLE
130.

SEX AND HIP FRACTURE
065.

SEX HORMONE BINDING GLOBULINS
130.

SEXUAL ABUSE, CHILDHOOD; EFFECTS OF
145.

SEXUAL ASSAULT HISTORY
131.

SEXUAL BEHAVIOR
173.

SEXUAL RISK, HIV
067.

SEXUAL RISK REDUCTION, HIV
068.

SEXUALITY KNOWLEDGE
125.

SEXUALLY TRANSMITTED DISEASES
132.

SEXUALLY TRANSMITTED INFECTION
173.

SHEA DG ET AL
146.

SHORT FORM HEALTH SURVEY
002.

SIGMOID VOLVULUS
133.

SIGNS OF STROKE
174.

SINCLAIR L ET AL
187.

SLEEP PROBLEMS
029.

SMILING IN PRETERM INFANTS
134.

SMITH GD ET AL
135.

SMOKERS, AFRICAN AMERICAN
197.

SMOKING AMONG ADOLESCENTS
110.

SMOKING AND STOMACH CANCER RISK
136.

SMOKING ASSISTANCE, PAST QUIT
094.

SMOKING BURDEN AND MORTALITY
140.

SMOKING, PASSIVE
093.

SMYTH K ET AL
053.

SOCIAL ACCEPTANCE
151.

SOCIAL CLASS, LOWER, AND HEART DISEASE
194.

SOCIAL ENVIRONMENT & SUBSTANCE MIS-USE
143.

SOCIAL FACTORS: HYPERTENSION
070.

SOCIAL INTERACTIONS
060.

SOCIAL RESPONSIBILITY
082.

SOCIAL SUPPORT, PERCEIVED
096.

SOCIETAL BARRIERS IN PSYCHOTHERAPY
012.

SOCIO-DEMOGRAPHICS: WOMEN: HIV-AIDS
177.

SOCIO-DEMOGRAPHY WOMEN: MAMMOGRAPHY
080.

SOCIO-ECONOMIC AFR-AM: MEDICATIONS
076.

SOCIO-ECONOMIC DIFFERENTIALS
135.

SOCIO-ECONOMIC STATUS & SLEEP PROBL
029.

SOCIO-ECONOMIC STATUS AND DEPRESSION
034.

SOUTH AFRICAN GOLD MINERS
091.

SOUTH AFRICANS: APPENDICITIS
007.

SPENCE SA ET AL
052.

STAKE FOR HEALTH OF AFRICAN-AM
199.

STANTON BF ET AL
004.

STANTON BF ET AL
132.

STATISTICS, CANCER
026.

STEINBROOK R
040.

STEREOTYPES, CONFLICTING
187.

STILL-FACE SITUATION
134.

STOMACH CANCER RISK: MEN AND WOMEN
136.

STONE BA
180.

STRAKER G ET AL
157.

STRATEGIES, COPING;   MOTHERS
122.

STRATEGIES, INNOVATIVE
120.

STRESS, RESPONSE TO
113.

STRICKLAND WJ ET AL
032.

STROKE, SIGNS OF
174.

STRUCTURAL VARIABLES: INFANT MORTALITY
129.

STRUCTURE OF INFORMAL CARE
152.

STUDENTS, PERCEPTIONS TO SCHOOL, ETC
098.

STUDENTS, UNIVERSITY; KNOWLEDGE
125.

SUBSTANCE ABUSE AND RISK
057.

SUBSTANCE MIS-USE
143.

SUBSTANCE USE DISORDERS, PTSD & VICTIMIZ
156.

SUFFERING, PTSD
109.

SUPPORT, SOCIAL
096.

SURGERY, BYPASS
008.

SURGERY FOR COLORECTAL CANCER
137.

SURROGATE LAWS
139.

SURVEY: BREAST SCREENING
024.

SURVIVAL, CANCER
163.

SURVIVAL, RENAL DISEASE
087.

SURVIVAL: COLORECTAL CANCER
137.

SYMPTOMS, EATING DISORDERS
131.

SYNDROME CRISIS: HIV-AIDS
195.

SYNDROME, METABOLIC
079.

SYSTEMIC EXPOSURE TO COTININE
093.

TAYLOR RD ET AL
075.

TEJEDA HA ET AL
126.

TERESI JA ET AL
174.

TEST SCORES, INTELLIGENCE
047.

THERAPEUTICS FOR WOMEN WITH HIV
013.

THERAPY, GROUP
061.

TIMING, FERTILITY
175.

TISSUE DONATION: PROBLEM AND SOLUTION
170.

TOBACCO CONTROL
088.

TOMAINO-BRUNNER C ET AL
001.

TRANS-RACIAL ADOPTION DEBATE
057.

TRANSPLANTATION, RENAL
192.

TRAUMA: YOUNG BLACK MALES
160.

TREATING AFRICAN AMERICANS
107.

TREATMENT DIFFERENCES
108.

TREATMENT FOR PEOPLE OF COLOR
061.

TREATMENT FOR PTSD
118.

TREATMENT OF COCAINE ADDICTION
051.

TREATMENT ORGANIZATIONS; SUBSTANCE
143.

TREATMENT OUTCOMES, COCAINE
106.

TREATMENTS FOR COCAINE ABUSE
106.

TRENDS IN US BLACK INFANT MORTALITY
154.

TRIAL OF AIDS PREVENTION PROGRAM
004.

TRIALS, NCI: REPRESENTATION IN
126.

TROCHANTERIC FRACTURES: US ELDERLY
065.

TSC2 GENE
088.

TUSKEGEE
171.

TYPE, BODY
115.

TYPE II DIABETES
033.

TYPE II DIABETES; MANAGEMENT
036.

U.S. BLACK & WHITES: ALCOHOL & CANCER
015.

U.S. METRO AREAS: SEGREGATION IN
077.

U.S.: ANDROGENS AND LIFE STYLE FACTORS
130.

U.S.: BLACK IDENTITY AND DRINKING
021.

UNIVERSITY STUDENTS
125.

NICHOLAS L ET AL
125.

URBAN ADOLESCENTS, STD, HIB, ETC
132.

URBAN DIABETES
036.

URINARY PROBLEMS AS A PREDICTOR
182.

URINE ANALYSIS AND SMOKING
093.

US ADOLESCENTS; SMOKING
110.

US ELDERLY: FRACTURES
065.

US WOMEN: HYPERTENSION, PREG & COMPL
081.

US: MEDICAL CARE EMPLOYMENT
084.

USA: SAFE MOTHERHOOD
181.

USE, ALCOHOL AND CANCER RISK
015.

USE, MAMMOGRAPHY
080.

USERS, DRUG
183.

VALUES, HEALTH
003.

VAN RENSBURG EJ ET AL
035.

VARIATION IN FERTILITY TIMING
175.

VARICELLA
116.

**VEAL YS
010.**

**VEAL YS
003.**

**VEAL YS
063.**

**VETERANS, COMBAT
118.**

**VETERANS SUFFERING PTSD
109.**

**VICTIM INJURY
100.**

**VICTIMIZATION AND PTSD
156.**

**VIOLENCE AND COPING
122.**

**VIOLENCE AND RACE
100.**

**VIOLENCE, DOMESTIC
100.**

**VIOLENT POTENTIAL CONTEXTS; YOUTH
157.**

**VOCATIONAL CAREER AND DRUGS
141.**

VOICES FOR HEALTH CARE
003.

VOLVULUS, SIGMOID
133.

VULNERABILITY TO UNEMPLOYMENT
113.

WAIT-LIST: AFRO-AM; KIDNEYS
016.

WALKING:EFFECT ON DISABILITY
144.

WARDLOW H ET AL
128.

WAYS OF COPING QUESTIONNAIRE
053.

WEIGHT, INFANT BIRTH
006.

WEIGHT MODIFICATION EFFORTS
158.

WEINRICH SP ET AL
182.

WELCH J ET AL
190.

WELLBEING IN DISADVANTAGED FAMILIES
075.

WHITE MEN AND ANDROGENS
130.

WHITE MEN AND WOMEN: DISADVANTAGED
002.

WHITE WOMEN: MEASURE OF PHYSICAL ACTIV
083.

WHITE WOMEN: POLITICAL PARTICIPATION
082.

WHITE WOMEN; DEPRESSION
034.

WHITES & REPRESENTATION IN NCI TRIALS
126.

WHITES AND AFR-AM: METABOLIC SYNDROME
079.

WILLIAMS JE ET AL
168.

WILLIAMS JK
013.

WINETT RA ET AL
067.

WINGO PA ET AL
026.

WOHL AR ET AL
177.

WOLINSKY FD ET AL
002.

WOMEN, ADJUSTMENT TO MASTECTOMY
096.

WOMEN, AIDS-HIV
177.

WOMEN AND AIDS
159.

WOMEN AND BREAST CANCER
023.

WOMEN AND HEATH CARE SECTOR JOBS
084.

WOMEN AND HIV RISK REDUCTION INTERVENT
067.

WOMEN AND HYPERTENSION
046.

WOMEN AND MEN
002.

WOMEN AND MEN IN RETIREMENT
099.

WOMEN AND MEN: SEX ASSAULT HISTORY, ET
131.

WOMEN, BLACK: CHD MORE RISK IN
176.

WOMEN, DIVERSE: MAMMOGRAPHY
080.

WOMEN, HIGH RISK: AIDS PREVENTION
014.

WOMEN IN PSYCHOTHERAPY
012.

WOMEN, INNER-CITY: INJURIES
073.

WOMEN LIVING WITH HIV
013.

WOMEN, METHADONE DEPENDENT
097.

WOMEN, MINORITY
001.

WOMEN, OBESE
083.

WOMEN RECEIVE LESS MAMMOGRAPHY
022.

WOMEN, US: HYPERTENSION, PREG, COMPL
081.

WOMEN, WHITE
176.

WOMEN: BODY TYPE PREFERENCES
115.

WOMEN: DEPRESSION IN
034.

WOMEN: HIV RISK REDUCTION INTERVENTION
068.

WOMEN: MENTAL HEALTH ISSUES
085.

WOMEN: POLITICAL PARTICIPATION
082.

WOMEN: STOMACH CANCER RISK
136.

WOMEN: WAYS OF COPING QUESTIONNAIRE
053.

WORKERS AND ATTITUDES; HEALTH CARE
049.

WORKING AND 'DRUGGING' IN THE CITY
193.

WU, AH ET AL
130.

YOOS HL ET AL
027.

YOUTH AND LOW INCOME
066.

YOUTH, LOW INCOME
066.

YOUTH: EMOTIONAL CONCERNS OF 157.

ZAPKA JG ET AL 080.

ZIEMER DC ET AL 036.

<><>

BIBLIOGRAPHICAL REFERENCES

001
"I hope I don't have cancer": colposcopy and minority women.
Tomaino-Brunner C et al
Oncol Nurs Forum 1996 Jan-Feb; 23 (1) 39-44.

002
A measurement model of the Medical Outcomes study: 36-Item Short-Form Health Survey in a clinical sample of disadvantaged, older, black and white men and women.
Wolinsky FD et al
Med Care 1996 Jun; 34 (6) 537-48.

003
A million voices for health care: strengthening the health values and behaviors of African Americans.
Veal YS
J Nat Med Assoc 1996 Jan; 88 (1) 13-4.

004
A randomized controlled effectiveness trial of an AIDS prevention program for low-income African-American youths.
Stanton BF et al
Arch Pediatr Adolesc Med 1996 Apr; 150 (4) 363-72.
43 References.

005
Abnormal eating attitudes and behaviors in two ethnic groups from a female British urban population.
Reiss D
Psychol Med 1996 Mar; 26 (2) 289-99.

006
Abuse during pregnancy: associations with maternal health and infant birth weight.
McFarlane J et al
Nurs Res 1996 Jan-Feb; 45 (1) 37-42.

007
Acute appendicitis among black South Africans.
Fulton J et al
S Afr J Surg 1995 Dec; 33 (4) 165-6.

008
Adverse 5-year outcome after coronary artery bypass surgery in blacks.
Gray RJ et al
Arch Intern Med 1996 Apr 8; 156 (7) 769-73.

009
Affirmative action politics: the shotgun plan revisited. Editorial.
Dawson G
J Natl Med Assoc 1995 Dec; 87 (12) 853-6.

010
African Americans and diabetes: reasons, rationale and research.
Veal YS
J Natl Med Assoc 1996 Apr; 88 (4) 203-4.

011
African-American adolescents residing in high-risk urban environments do use condoms: correlates and predictors of condom use among adolescents in public housing developments.
Di Clemente RJ et al
Pediatrics 1996 Aug; 98 (2 pt 1) 269-78.

012
African-American women: considering diverse identities and societal barriers in psychotherapy.
Greene B
Ann NY Acad Sci 196 Jun 18; 789:191-209.
30 References.

013
Afro-American women living with HIV infection: special therapeutic interventions for a growing population.
Williams JK
Soc Work Health Care 1995; 21 (2) 41-53.
30 References.

014
AIDS prevention in high-risk African American women: behavioral, psychological and gender issues.
Hetherington SE et al
J Sex Marital Ther 1996 Spring; 22 (1) 9-21.

015
Alcohol use and prostate cancer risk in U.S. Blacks and whites.
Hayes RB et al
Am J Epidemiol 1996 Apr 1; 143 (7) 692-7.

016
Allocation of kidneys to Afro-American patients proportional to wait-list composition.
Bryan CF et al
Transplant Proc 1996 Feb; 28 (1) 219-20.

017
an empowerment-centered, church-based asthma education program for African American adults.

Ford ME et al
Health Soc Work 1996 Feb; 21 (1) 70-5.

018
An exploratory study of African American collegiate adult children of alcoholics.
Rodney HE et al
J Am Coll Health 1996 May; 44 (6) 267-72.

019
Anthropolology's Hoodoo Museum.
Fox K
Cut Med Psychiatry 1995 Sep; 19 (3) 409-21.

020
Attitudes of African-Americans regarding screening for prostate cancer.
Robinson SB et al
J Natl Med Assoc 1996 Apr; 88 (4) 241-6.

021
Black identity and drinking in the US: a national study.
Herd D et al
Addiction 1996 Jun; 91 (6) 845-57.

022
Black women receive less mammography even with similar use of primary care. Comments.
Burns RB et al
Ann Intern Med 1995 Aug 1; 125 (3) 173-82. Comment in AIM 1996 Aug 1; 125 (3) 237-9.

023
Breast cancer and black women.
Moormeier J
Ann Intern Med 1996 May 15; 124 (10) 897-905.
98 References.

024
Breast screening by African American women: insights from a house-hold survey and focus groups.
Danigelis NL et al
Am J Prev Med 1995 Sep-Oct; 11 (5) 31-7.

025
Cancer fatalism among African-americans: a review of the literature.
Powe BD
Nurs Outlook 1996 Jan-Feb;44 (1) 18-21.
25 References.

026
Cancer statistics for African Americans, 1996.
Wingo PA et al
CA Cancer J Clin 1996 Mar-apr;46 (2) 113-25.

027
Child rearing beliefs in the African-American community: implications for culturally competent pediatric care.
Yoos HL et al
J Pediatr Nurs 1995 Dec; 10 (6) 343-53.
73 References.

028
Clinical characteristics of black asthmatic children.
Luyt DK et al
S Afr Med J 1995; Oct; 85 (10) 999-1001.

029
Co-sleeping and early childhood sleep problems: effects of ethnicity and socio-economic status.
Lozoff B et al
J Dev Behav Pediatr 1996 Feb; 17 (1) 9-15.

030
Cognitive and family-support mediators of preschool effectiveness; a confirmatory analysis.
Reynolds AJ et al
Child Dev 1996 Jun; 67 (3) 1119-40.

031
Coping diabetes and the older African-American.
Degazon CD
Nurs Outlook 1995 Nov-Dec; 43 (6) 254-9.

032
Coping with the cost of prescription drugs.
Strickland WJ et al
J Health Care Poor Underserved 1996; 7 (1) 50-62.

033
Decreased insulin-mediated but not non-insulin-dependent glucose disposal rates in glucose intolerance and type II diabetes in African (Ghanaian) immigrants.
Osei K et al
Am J Med Sci 1996 Mar; 311 (3) 113-21.

034
Depression in black and white women. The role of marriage and socio-economic status.
Gazmararian JA et al
Ann Epidemiol 1995 Nov; 5 (6) 455-63.

035
Detection of human papillomavirus DNA with in situ hybridization in oral squamous carcinoma in a rural black population.
Van Rensburg EJ et al
S Afr Med J 1995 Sep; 85 (9) 894-6.

036
Diabetes in urban African Americans. III. Management of type II diabetes in a municipal hospital setting.
Ziemer DC et al
Am J Med 1996 Jul; 101 (1)25-33.

037
Digital rectal examinations and prostate cancer screening: attitudes of African American men.
Gelfand DE et al
Oncol Nurs Forum 1995 Sep; 22 (8) 1253-5.

038
Dis-entangling the effects of disability status and gender on the labor supply of Anglo, black and Latino older workers.
Santiago AM et al
Gerontologist 1996 Jun; 36 (3) 299-310.

039
Dismantling discrimination in dental education.
Dummett CO
J Natl Med Assoc 1996 Jul; 88 (7) 454-9.

040
Diversity in medicine. Editorial, comment.
Steinbrook R
N Engl J Med 1996 May 16; 234 (20) 1327-8. Comment on: NEJM May 16; 234 (20) 1305-10.

041
Do African-Americans wait longer for a kidney because of HLA class I antibody specificities and pane-reactive antibody sensitization?
Luger AM et al
Transplant Proc 1996 Feb; 28 (1) 157-9.

042
Eating disturbances among American minority groups: a review.
Crago M et al
Int J Eat Disord 1996 Apr; 19 (3) 239-48.
59 References.

043
Educating African-Americans about cancer prevention and detection: a review of the literature.
Lowe JI et al
Soc Work Health Care 1995; 21 (4) 17-36.
36 References.

044
Effect of air pollution on african-American and other minority populations.
Olden K
Otolaryngol Head Neck Surg 1996 Feb;114 (2)255.

045
Epidemiology of high grade prostatic intra-epithelial neoplasia.
Sakr WA et al
Pathol Res Pract 1995 Sep; 191 (9) 838-41.

046
Epidemiology of hypertension in African American women.
Gillum RF
Am Heart J 1996 Feb; 131 (2) 385-95.
72 References.

047
Ethnic differences in children's intelligence test scores: role of economic deprivation, home

environment and maternal characteristics.
Brooks-Gunn J et al
Child Dev 1996 Apr; 67 (2) 396-408.

048
Ethnic groups.
Millar J et al
Prim Care 1995 Dec; 22 (4) 713-20.
27 References.

049
Ethnically sensitive messengers: an exploration of racial attitudes of health-care workers and organ procurement officers.
Mitchell AA et al
J Natl Med Assoc 1996 Jun; 88 (6) 349-52.

050
Ethnicity and psychotherapy. A component in the treatment of cocaine addiction in African Americans.
Foulks EF et al
Psychiatr Clin North Am 1995 Sep; 18 (3) 607-20.
59 References.

051
Evidence for recent growth of the HIV epidemic among African-American men and younger male cohorts in Los Angeles County.
Greenland S et al
J Acquir Immune Defic Syndr Hum Retrovirol 1996 Apr 1; 11 (4) 401-9.

052
Exploring the relationship between purpose in life and African American adolescents' use of prenatal

care services.
Spence SA et al
Soc Work Health Care 1995; 22 (2) 43-53.

053
Factor analysis of the Ways of Coping Questionnaire for African American women.
Smyth K et al
Nurs Res 1996 Jan-Feb; 45 (1) 25-9.

054
Factors associated with intention to undergo annual prostate cancer screening among African American men in Philadelphia.
Myers RE et al
Cancer 1996 Aug 1; 78 (3) 471-9.

055
Factors predicting change in prescription and non-prescription drug use in a community-residing black and white elderly population.
Fillenbaum GG et al
J Clin Epidemiol 1996 May; 49(5) 587-93.

056
Fewer black kidney donors: what's the problem?
Griffin LW et al
Soc Work Health Care 1995; 22 (2) 19-42.

057
Forensic and policy implications of the trans-racial adoption debate.
Griffith EE
Bull Am Acad Psychiatry Law 1995 23 (4) 501-12.

058
Gender differences in early life risk factors for substance use/abuse: a study of an African-American sample.
Friedman AS et al
Am J Drug Alcohol Abuse 1995 Nov; 21 (4)511-31.

059
Gender differences on the Outcome Questionnaire.
Nebeker RS et al
Psychol Rep 1995 Dec; 77 (3 pt 1) 875-9.

060
Gender patterns in African American and white adolescents' social interactions in same-race, mixed-gender groups.
Filardo EK
J Pers Soc Psychol 1996 Jul; 71 (1) 71-82.

061
Group therapy as an effective treatment modality for people of color.
Fenster A
Int J group Psychother 1996 Jul; 46 (3) 399-416.
42 References.

062
Have we succeeded in reducing barriers to medical care for African and Hispanic Americans with Disabilities?
Cornelius LJ et al
Soc Work Health Care 195; 22 (2) 1-17.

063
Health care in the African-American community. A chronology of successes, an examination of

realities and a hope for remedies.
Veal YS
J natl Med Assoc 1996 May; 88 (5) 265-7.

064
Heeding the alcoholic beverage warning label during pregnancy: multi-parae versus nulliparae.
Hankin JR et al
J Stud Alcohol 1996 Mar; 57 (2) 171-7.

065
Heterogeneity of hip fracture: age, race, sex and geographic patterns of femoral neck and trochanteric fractures among the US elderly.
Karagas MR et al
Am J Epidemol 1996 Apr 1; 143 (7) 677-82.

066
Heterosexual experiences and partnerships of urban, low-income African-American and Hispanic youth.
Norris AE et al
J Acquir Immune Defic Syndr Hum Retrovirol 1996 Mar 1; 11 (3) 288-300.

067
HIV sexual risk-reduction intervention for African-American women. Letter.
Winett RA et al
JAMA 1996 Feb 28; 275 (8); 593; discussion 594-5.

068
HIV sexual risk-reduction interventions for African-American women. Letter.
Branson BM et al

JAMA 1996 Feb 28; 275 (8) 593-4; discussion 594-5.

069
HLA-DQ3 is associated with Graves' disease in African-Americans.
Ofosu MH et al
Immunol Invest 1996 Jan-Mar; 25 (1-2) 103-10.

070
Hypertension in the African American community: social, cultural and psychological factors.
Dressler WW
Semin Nephrol 1996 Mar; 16 (2) 71-82.
52 References.

071
Inconsistencies in the literature on collegiate adult children of alcoholics: factors to consider for African Americans.
Rodney HE
J Am Coll Health 1996 Jul; 45 (1) 19-25.
58 References.

072
Infant mortality in Caucasians and African Americans.
Lester D
Psychol Rep 1995 Dec; 77 (3 pt 1) 962.

073
Injuries among inner-city minority women: a population-based longitudinal study.
Grisso JA et al
Am J Public Health 1996 Jan; 86 (1) 67-70.

074
Kidney disease in the first-degree relatives of African-Americans with hypertensive end-stage renal disease.
Bergman S et al
Am J Kidney Dis 1996 Mar; 27 (3) 341-6.

075
Kinship support and maternal and adolescent well-being in economically disadvantaged African-American families.
Taylor RD et al
Child Dev 1995 Dec; 66 (6) 1585-97.

076
Knowledge, beliefs and use of prescribed antibiotic medications among low socio-economic African-Americans.
Kandakai TL et al
J Natl Med Assoc 1996 May; 88 (5) 298-94.

077
Latino, Asian and black segregation in U.S. metropolitan areas: are multi-ethnic metros different?
Frey WH et al
Demography 1996 Feb; 33 (1) 35-50.

078
Life events and hypertension--a negative finding.
Edwards D
S Afr Med J 1995 Dec;85 (12 pt 2) 1346-8.

079
A metabolic syndrome in whites and African-Americans. The Atherosclerosis Risk in

Communities baseline study.
Schmidt MI et al
Diabetes Care 1996 May 19 (5) 409-13.

080
Mammography use among socio-demographically diverse women: the accuracy of self-report.
Zapka JG et al
Am J Public Health 1996 Jul; 86 (7) 1016-21.

081
Maternal hypertension and associated pregnancy complications among African-American and other women in the United States.
Samadi AR et al
Ob Gynecol 1996 Apr; 87 (4) 557-63.

082
Meanings of political participation among black and white women: political identity and social responsibility.
Cole ER et al
J Pers Soc Psychol 1996 Jul; 71 (1) 130-40.

083
Measurement of physical activity among black and white obese women.
Kushner RF et al
Obes Res 1995 Sep; 3 suppl 2: 261s-265s.

084
Medical care employment in the United States, 1968 to 1993: The importance of health sector jobs for African Americans and women.
Himmelstein DU et al
Am J Public Health 1996 Apr; 86(4) 525-8.

085
Mental health issues in African-American women.
Chisholm JF
Ann NY Acad Sci 1996 Jun 18; 789:161-79.

086
Minorities in medicine: the Flexner Report . Letter.
Hasbrouck LM
JAMA 1996 May 22-29; 275 (20) 1547-8.

087
Minority advantage in diabetic end-stage renal disease survival on hemodialysis: due to different proportions of diabetic type?
Medina RA et al
Am J Kidney Dis 1996 Aug; 28 (2) 226-34.

088
Mobilizing a low-income African American community around tobacco control: a force field analysis.
Ellis GA et al
Health Educ Q 1995 Nov; 22 (4) 443-57.

089
Mutation-analysis of the TSC2 gene in an African-American family.
Kumar A et al
Hum Mol Genet 1995 Dec; 4 (12) 2295-8.

090
Nutritional risk in inner-city dwelling older black Americans.
Miller DK et al
J Am Geriatr Soc 1996 Aug; 44 (8) 959-62.

091
Occupational disease trends in black South African gold miners. an autopsy-based study.
Murray J et al
Am J Respir Crit Care Med 1996 Feb; 153 (2) 706-10.

092
Outreach: How race colors breast cancer.
Sandrick KM
Hosp Health Netw 1996 Jun 20; 70 (12) 68.

093
Passive smoking in children. Racial differences in systemic exposure to cotinine by hair and urine analysis.
Knight JM et al
Chest 1996 Feb; 109 (2) 446-50.

094
Past quit smoking assistance and doctors' advice for white and African-American smokers.
Hymowitz N et al
J Natl Med Assoc 1996 Apr; 88 (4) 249-52.

095
Perceived health, HIV illness and mental distress in African-American clients of AIDS counseling centers.
Linn JG et al
J Assoc Nurses AIDS Care 1996 Mar-Apr; 7 (2) 43-51.

096
Perceived social support and adjustment to mastectomy in socio-economically disadvantaged

black women.
Beder J
Soc Work Health Care 1995; 22 (2) 55-71.

097
Perception of AIDS risk and high-risk behaviors in African-American methadone-dependent women.
Harris RM et al
AIDS Educ Prev 1995 Oct; 7 (5)415-28.

098
Perceptions and attitudes of black students toward school, achievement, and other eductional variables.
Ford DY et al
Child Dev 1996 Jun; 67 (3) 1141-52.

099
Physical function among retirement-aged African American men and women.
Clark DO et al
Gerontologist 1996 Jun; 36 (3) 322-31.

100
Police involvement in domestic violence: the interactive effects of victim injury, offenders's history of violence and race.
Bachman R et al
Violence 1995 Summer; 10 (2) 91-106.

101
Pre- and peri-natal risk factors for asthma in inner city African-American children.
Oliveti JF et al
Am J Epidemiol 1996 Mar 15;143 (6) 570-7.

102
Preliminary observations on the relationship between mutans streptococci and dental caries experience within black, white and Hispanic families living in Houston, Texas.
Korenstein K et al
Pediatr Dent 1995 Nov-Dec; 17 (7) 445-50.

103
Preterm birth in the African American community.
Hogue CJ et al
Semin Perinatol 1995 Aug; 19 (4) 255-62.
70 References.

104
Psychiatric disorders in African American nursing home residents.
Class CA et al
Am J Psychiatry 1996 May; 153 (5) 677-81.

105
Psychosocial outcomes of HIV illness in male and female African American clients.
Linn JG et al
Soc Work Health Care 1995; 21 (3) 43-60.

106
Psychosocial treatments for cocaine abuse. 12-month treatment outcomes.
Hoffman JA et al
J Subst Abuse Treat 1996 Jan-Feb; 13 (1) 3-11.

107
Psychosocial-cultural issues in medicine and psychiatry: treating African-Americans.
Carter JH
J Natl Med Assoc 1995 Dec; 87(12) 857-60. 18 Ref.

108
Race and gender differences in the treatment of psychiatric disorders in young adolescents.
Cuffe SP et al
J Am Acad Child Adolesc Psychiatry 1995 Nov; 34 (11) 1536-43.

109
Race and outcome of treatment for veterans suffering from PTSD.
Rosenheck R et al
J Trauma Stress 1996 Apr; 9 (2) 343-51.

110
Race and the incidence of cigarette smoking among adolescents in the United States.
Faulkner DL et al
J Natl Cancer inst 1996 Aug 21; 88 (16) 1158-60.

111
Race differences in labor force attachment and disability status.
Bound J et al
Gerontologist 1996 Jun; 36 (3) 311-21.

112
Race, gender and opportunity: a study of compensation attainment and the establishment of mentoring relationships.
Dreher GF et al
J Appl Psychol 1996 Jun; 81 (3) 297-308.

113
Race, gender and the response to stress: auto-workers' vulnerability to long-term unemployment.
Broman CL et al
Am J Community Psychol 1995 Dec; 23 (6) 813-42.

114
Race inequities in men's retirement.
Hayward MD et al
J Gerontol B Psychol Sci Soc Sci 1996 Jan; 51 (1) s1-10.

115
Racial differences in Body type preferences of men for women.
Greenberg DR et al
Int J Eat Disord 1996 Apr; 19 (3) 275-8.

116
Racial differences in herpes zoster and age at onset of varicella. Letter.
Dworkn RH
J Infect Dis 1996; Jul; 174 (1) 239-41.

117
Racial differences in home owner ship and home equity among pre-retirement-aged house-holds.
Myers SL Jr et al
Gerontologist 1996 Jun; 36 (3) 350-60.

118
Racial differences on psychological measures in combat veterans seeking treatment for PTSD.
Frueh BC et al
J Pers Assess 1996 Feb; 66 (1) 41-53.

119
Racial effects on the clinical presentation of alcoholics at a psychiatric hospital.
Cornelius JR et al
Compr Psychiatry 1996 Mar-Apr; 37 (2) 102-8.

120
Reaching out to the African American community through innovative strategies.
Robinson KD et al
Oncol Nurs Forum 1995 Oct; 22 (9) 1383-91.
28 References.

121
Relation of maternal race to the risk of preterm, non-low birth weight infants: a population study.
Collins JW Jr et al
Am J Epidemiol 1996 Feb 15; 143 (4) 333-7.

122
Relationship between multiple exposures to violence and coping strategies among African American mothers.
Hill HM et al
Violence Vict 1995 Spring 10 (1) 55-71.

123
Relationship of age, education and occupation with dementia among a community-based sample of African Americans.
Callahan CM et al
Arch Neurol 1996 Feb;53 (2) 134-40.

124
Relevance of race or ethnic group in case reports.
Letter.
Mosby JA
Am Fam Physician 1996 Apr; 53 (5) 1530.

125
Religiosity, AIDS and sexuality knowledge, attitudes, beliefs and practices of black South-

African first-year university students.
Nicholas L et al
Psychol Rep 1995 Dec; 77 (3 pt 2) 1328-30.

126
Representation of African-Americans, Hispanics and whites in National Cancer Institute treatment trials.
Tejeda HA et al
J Natl Cancer Inst 1996 Jun 19; 88 (12) 812-6.

127
Role of dietary factors in the hypertension of African Americans.
Adrogue HJ et al
Semin Nephrol 1996 Mar; 16 (2) 94-101.
45 References.

128
'Sympathy for my body' : breast cancer and mammography at two Atlanta clinics.
Wardlow H et al
Med Anthropol 1996 Mar; 16 (4) 319-40.

129
Separate black and white infant mortality models: differences in the importance of structural variables.
Bird ST
Soc Sci Med 1995 Dec; 41 (11) 1507-12.
37 References.

130
Serum androgens and sex hormone-binding globulins in relation to life-style factors in older African-American, white, and Asian men in the

United States and Canada.
Wu, AH et al
Cancer Epidemiol Biomarkers Prev 1995 Oct-Nov; 4 (7) 735-41.

131
Sexual assault history and eating disorder symptoms among White, Hispanic and African-American women and men.
Laws A et al
Am J Public Health 1996 Apr; 86 (4) 579-82.

132
Sexually transmitted diseases, human immuno-deficiency virus and pregnancy prevention. Combined contraceptive practices among urban African American early adolescents.
Stanton BF et al
Arch Pediat Adolesc Med 1996 Jan; 150 (1) 17-24.

133
Sigmoid volvulus among Africans in Durban.
Mokoena TR et al
Trop Georg Med 1995; 47 (5) 216-7.

134
Smiling and fussing in seven-moth-old preterm and full-term black infants in the still-face situation.
Segal LB et al
Child Dev 1995 Dec; 66 (6) 1829-43.

135
Socio-economic differentials in mortality risk among men screened for the Multiple Risk Factor Intervention Trial: II. Black men.
Smith GD et al
Am J Public Health 1996 Apr; 86 (4) 497-504.

136
Stomach cancer risk among black and white men and women: the role of occupation and cigarette smoking.
Burns PB et al
J Occup Environ Med 1995 Oct; 37 (10) 1218-23.

137
Surgery for colorectal cancer; Race-related differences in rates and survival among Medicare beneficiaries.
Cooper GS et al
Am J Public Health 1996 Apr; 86 (4) 582-6.

138
Targeted chemotherapy for parasite infestations in rural black preschool children.
Taylor M et al
S Afr Med J 1995 Sep; 85 (9) 870-4.

139
The application of health care surrogate laws to older populations: how good a match?
Hayley DC et al
J Am Geriatr Soc 1996 Feb; 44 (2) 185-8.

140
The burden of smoking--attributable mortality among African Americans--Indiana, 1990.
Emont SL et al
Addict Behav 1995 Sep-Oct; 20 (5) 563-9.

141
The consequences of drug use/abuse for vocational career: a longitudinal study of male urban African-American sample.
Friedman AS et al
Am J Drug Alcohol Abuse 1996; Feb;22(1) 57-73.

142
The dis-proportionate impact of environmental health threats on children of color.
Mott L
Environ Health Perspect 1995 Sep; 103 suppl 6: 33-5.

143
The effect of social environment of treatment outcomes in outpatient substance misuse treatment organizations: does race really matter?
Howard DL et al
Subst Use Misuse 1996 Apr; 31 (5) 617-38.

144
The effect of walking on lower body disability among older blacks and whites.
Clark DO
Am J Public Health 1996 Jan; 86 (1) 57-61.

145
The effects of childhood sexual abuse on minority adolescent mothers.
Esparza DV et al
J Ob Gynecol Neonatal Nurs 1996 May; 25 (4) 321.

146
The health-wealth connection: racial differences.
Shea DG et al
Gerontologist 1996 Jun; 36 (3) 342-9.

147
The inter-generational relationship between mother's birth-weight, infant birth-weight and infant mortality in black and white mothers.
Sanderson M et al
Pediatr Perinat Epidemiol 1995 Oct; 9 (4) 391-405.

148
The Julius Rosenwald fund syphilis seroprevalence studies.
Roy B
J Natl Med Assoc 1996 May; 88 (5) 315-22.

149
The perceptions of African-American physicians concerning their treatment of managed care organizations. Editorial.
Lavizzo-Mourey R et al
J Natl Med Assoc 1996 Apr; 88 (4) 210-4.

150
The Pictorial Scale of Perceived Competence and Social Acceptance: does it work with low-income urban children?
Fantuzzo JW et al
Child Dev 1996 Jun; 67 (3) 1071-84.

151
The role of black and Hispanic physicians in providing health care for underserved populations Comments.
Komaromy M et al
N Engl J Med 1996 May 16; 334 (20) 1305-10.
Comment in: NEJM May 16; 334 (20) 1327-8.

152
The structure of informal care: are there differences by race?
Burton L et al
Gerontologist 1995 Dec; 35 (6) 744-52.

153
Total joint arthroplasty in a predominantly African-american population. Part two: Hip arthroplasty.
Rankin EA et al
J Natl Med Assoc 1996;Apr; 88 (4) 233-6.

154
Trends in US urban black infant mortality by degree of residential segregation.
Polednak AP
Am J Public Health 1996 May; 86(5) 723-6.

155
Use of educational resource materials with South African children in day care.
Liddell C
Psychol Rep 1995 Dec; 77 (3 pt 2) 1159-68.

156
Victimization and PTSD in individuals with substance use disorders: gender and racial differences.
Dansky BS et al
Am J Drug Alcohol Abuse 1996 Feb; 22 (1) 75-93.

157
Violent potential contexts and the emotional concerns of township youth.
Straker G et al
Child Dev 1996 Feb; 67 (1) 46-54.

158
Weight modification efforts reported by black and white pre-adolescent girls: National Heart, Lung and Blood Institute Growth and Health Study.
Schreiber GB et al
Pediatrics 1996 Jul; 98 (1) 63-70.

159
What African-American women know, do and feel about AIDS: a function of age and education.
Dancy B
AIDS Educ Prev 1996 Feb; 8 (1) 26-36.

160
Young black males and trauma: pre-disposing factors to presentation in an urban trauma unit.
Godbold DT et al
J Natl Med Assoc 1996 May; 88(5) 273-5.

161.
Race and outcomes: is this the end of the beginning for minority health research? Editorial, comment.
Brawley OW et al
J Nat Cancer Inst 1999 November 17; 91 (22) 1908-9.
Comment on: 91 (22) 1433-40.

162.
Outcomes among African-Americans and Caucasians in colon cancer adjuvant therapy trials: findings from the National Surgical Adjuvant Breast and Bowel Project. Comments.
Dignam JJ et al
J Natl Cancer Inst 1999 November 17; 91 (22) 19-33--40. Comment in 91 (22) 1908-9.

163.
Racial gaps in cancer survival: asking the wrong questions?
Kuska B
J Natl Cancer Inst 1999 November 17; 91 (22) 1912-3.

164.
Race and clinical outcome in endometrial carcinoma.
Cornell PP et al
Obstet Gynecol 1999 November; 94 (5 pt 1) 12-20.

165.
Alcohol consumption and changes in blood pressure among African Americans. The Pint County Study.
Cutis A et al
Am J Epidemiol 1997 November 1; 146 (9) 727-33.

166.
Racial and gender differences in use of procedures for black and white hospitalized adults.
Harris DR et al
Ethn Dis 1997 Spring-Summer; 7 (2) 91-105.

167.
Examination of racial differences in management of cardiovascular disease.
Ferguson JA et al
J Am Coll Cardiol 1997 December; 30 (7) 1707-13.

168.
Racial disparities in CHD mortality from 1968-1992 in the state economic areas surrounding the ARIC study communities. Atherosclerosis Risk in Communities.
Williams JE et al
Ann Epidemiol 1999 November; 9 (8) 472-80.

169.
Race, foster care and the politics of abandonment in New York City. Comments.
Rosner D et al
Am J Public Health 1997 November; 87 (11) 1844-9. Comment in: 87 (1) 1765-6.

170.
Organ / tissue donation the problem! Education the solution: a review.
Callender CO et al
J Natl Med Assoc 1997 October; 89 (10) 689-93.

171.
Under the shadow of Tuskegee: African Americans and health care. Comments.
Gamble VN
Am J Public Health 1997 November; 87 (11) 1773-8   Comment in: 87 (11) 1765-6.
47 References.

172.
Maternal psychological functioning, family processes and child adjustment in rural, single-parent, African American families.
Brody GH et al
Dev Psychol 1997 November; 33 (6) 1000-11.

173.
Sexual behavior and sexually transmitted infection among African and Caribbean men in London.
Evans BA et al
Int J STD AIDS 1999 November; 10 (11) 744-8.

174.
Use of latent class analyses for the estimation of prevalence of cognitive impairment and signs of stroke and Parkinson's disease among African American elderly of central Harlem: results of the Harlem Aging Project.
Teresi JA et al
Neuroepidemiology 1999; 18 6) 309-21.

175.
Health inequality and population variation in fertility-timing.
Geronimus AT et al
Soc Sci Med 1999 December; 49 (12)1623-36.

176.
Premenopausal black women have more risk factors for coronary heart disease than white women.
Gerhard GT et al
Am J Cardiol 1998 November 1; 82 (9) 1040-5.

177.
Socio-demographic and behavioral characteristics of African American women with HIV and AIDS in Los Angeles County, 1990-1997.
Wohl AR et al
J Acquir Immune Defic Syndr Hum Retrovirol 1998 December 1; 19 (4) 413-20.

178.
Ethnic differences in correlates of adolescent cigarette smoking.
Griesler PC et al
J Adolesc Health 1998 September; 23 (3) 167-80.

179.
Keynote address: prostate cancer among African American men--from the bench to the community.
Powell I
J Natl Med Assoc 1998 November; 90 (11 suppl) s705-9.

180.
Prostate cancer early detection in African American men: a priority for the 21st century.
Stone BA
J Nat Med Assoc 1998 November; 90 (11 suppl) s724-7.

181.
Safe motherhood USA. Editorial.
Lowe NK
J Ob Gynecol Neonatal Nurs 1998 September-October; 27 (5) 491.

182.
Urinary symptoms as a predictor for participation in prostate cancer screening among African American men.
Weinrich SP et al
Prostate 1998 December 1; 37 (4) 215-22.

183.
Help-seeking by African American drug users: a prospective analysis.
Longshore D
Addict Behav 1999 September-October; 24 (5) 683-6.

184.
Hair combing interactions: a new paradigm for research with African American mothers.
Lewis ML
Am J Orthopsychiatry 1999 October; 69 (4) 504-14.

185.
Linking maternal efficacy beliefs, developmental goals, parenting practices and child competence in rural single-parent African American families.
Brody GH et al
Child Dev 1999 September-October; 70 (5) 1197-208.

186.
African American female basketball players: an examination of alcohol and drug behaviors.
Bower BL et al
J Am Coll Health 1999 November; 48 (3) 129-33.

187.
Reactions to a black professional: motivated inhibition and activation of conflicting stereotypes.
Sinclair L et al
J Pers Soc Psychol 1999 November; 77 (5) 885-904.

188.
Age and intelligence as mediators of anger in black suicide attempters.
Lester D
Percept Mot Skills 1999 August; 8 (1) 338.

189.
Hispanics, Blacks and White driving under the influence of alcohol: results from the 1995 National Alcohol Survey.
Caetano R et al
Accid Anal Prev 2000 January; 32 (10 57-64.

190.
Quality of life in black hemodialysis patients.
Welch JL et al
Adv Ren Replace Ther 1999 October; 6 (4) 351-7.

191.
Association of school drop-out with recent and past injecting drug use among African American adults.
Obot IS et al
Addict Behav 1999 September-October;24 (5) 701-5.

192.
The effect of patients' preferences on racial differences in access to renal transplantation.
Ayanian JZ et al
N Engl J Med 1999 November 25; 341 (22) 1661-9.

193.
Working and "drugging" in the city: economics and substance use in a sample of working addicts.
Murdoch RO
Subst Use Misuse 1999 December; 34 (14) 2115-33.

194.
Evidence of increasing coronary heart disease mortality among black men of lower social class.

Comments.
Barnett E et al
Ann Epidemiol 1999 November; 9 (8) 461-3.

195.
Human immuno-deficiency virus / acquired immunodeficiency syndrome crisis.
Dennis GC
J Nat Med Assoc 1998 November; 90 (11) 643-4.

196.
Rapid progression to end-stage renal disease in young hypertensive African Americans with proteinuria.
Obialo CI et al
J Nat Med Assoc 1998 November; 90 (11) 649-55.

197.
Quit Today! A targeted communications campaign to increase use of the cancer information service by African American smokers.
Boyd NR et al
Prev Med 1998 September-October; 27 (5 pt 2) s50-60.

198.
The association of race / ethnicity, socio-economic status and physician recommendation for mammography:L who gets the message about breast cancer screening?
O'Malley MS et al
Am J Public Health 2001 January; 91 (1) 49-54.

199.
The November elections: what's at stake for the health of African Americans.
Hood RG
J Nat Med Assoc 2000 October; 92 (10) 461-3.

<><>

EPILOGUE AND FARE--THEE--WELL !

ATTITUDES MAY COME AND GO...

BUT POLITICS RUN THE SHOW..

BIBLIOGRAPHIC INFORMATION FOR ALL NATIONS

RESEARCH AND PROGRESS FOR ALL MANKIND

NEW REFERENCE BOOKS & RESEARCH INDEXES

OUR CONCERN IS YOUR HEALTH, AND THAT OF THE WORLD !

GOOD HEALTH IS OUR GREATEST WEALTH !
WHAT ARE WE, PERSON, BABY, CHILD OR COUNTRY
---WITHOUT GOOD HEALTH?
OUR INDEXES MAKE QUICK EXPERTS

* FAX ORDERS TO (703) 642-5966 ; E-MAIL: abbe.publishers@verizon.net

* OR WRITE TO: ABBE PUBLISHERS ASSOCIATION OF WASHINGTON, D.C.
4111 GALLOWS ROAD : VIRGINIA DIVISION
ANNANDALE, VIRGINIA USA 22003

BIOTERRORISM and Biology of Botulism (Clostridium Botulinum): Index of New Information and Guide-Book for Consumers, Reference and Research. December 2001. Cloth, 57.50: ISBN 0-7883-2710-0; PB is 50.50: ISBN 0-7883-2711-9. 175p. (See also title of Terrorism).

TERRORISM & Health Science Affairs: Index of New Information and Guide-Book for Consumers, Reference and Research. November 2001. Cloth, 57.50: ISBN 0-7883-2548-5; PB is 50.50: ISBN 0-7883-2549-3. 175p.

BIOTERRORISM OF SMALLPOX (Variola Virus): Index of New Information and Guide-Book for Consumers, Reference and Research. Nov 2001. Cloth, 57.50: ISBN 0-7883-2588-4; PB is 50.50: ISBN 0-7883-2589-2. 175p.

BIOTERRORISM OF PLAGUE (Yersinia Infections): Index of New Information and Guide-Book for Consumers, Reference and Research. November 2001. Cloth, 57.50: ISBN 0-7883-2630-9; PB is 50.50: ISBN 0-7883-2631-7. 175p.

BIOTERRORISM OF ANTHRAX (Bacillus anthracis): Index of New Information and Guide-Book for Consumers, Reference and Research. November 2001. Cloth, 57.50: ISBN 0-7883-2564-7; PB is 50.50: ISBN 0-7883-2565-5. 175p.

ABBE INDEXES QUICKLY CONNECT YOU TO THE WORLD LITERATURE

BE AN EXPERT WITH ABBE INDEXES

BIBLIOGRAPHIC INFORMATION FOR ALL NATIONS

RESEARCH AND PROGRESS FOR ALL MANKIND

NEW REFERENCE BOOKS & RESEARCH INDEXES

OUR BOOKS PROMOTE HEALTH & PEACE OF MIND

BIOTERRORISM, THREATS AND BIOLOGY OF TOXINS: Index of New Information and Guide-Book for Consumers, Reference and Research. December 2001. Cloth 57.50: ISBN 0-7883-2698-8; PB is 50.50: ISBN 0-7883-2699-6. 175p.

WAR --Analysis, Research, Policy and Politics with Progress: Index of New Information for Reference, Research and Archives. April 2002. Cloth 67.50: ISBN 0-7883-2430-6; PB is 57.50: ISBN 0-7883-2431-4. 175p.

Coenzyme Q - Ubiquinone: Index of New Information and Guide-Book for Consumers, Reference and Research. March 2002. Cloth 57.50: ISBN 0-7883-2498-5; PB is 47.50: 0-7883-2499-3; 175p.

Vitamin G - Riboflavin: Index of New Information and Guide-Book for Consumers, Reference and Research. March 2002. Cloth, 57.60; ISBN 0-7883-2486-1; PB is 47.50: ISBN 0-7883-2487-X. 175p.

Vitamin H - Biotin: Index of New Information and Guide-Book for Consumers, Reference and Research. April 2002. Cloth, 57.50: ISBN 0-7883-2504-3; PB is 47.50: ISBN 0-7883-2505-1. 175p.

Vitamin M - Folic Acid: Index of New Information and Guide-Book for Consumers, Reference and Research. June 2002. Cloth, 57.50; ISBN 0-7883-2506-X; PB is 47.50: ISBN 0-7883-2507-8. 175p.

Vitamin PP - Niacinamide: Index of New Information and Guide-Book for Consumers, Reference and Research. May 2002. Cloth, 57.50; ISBN 0-7883-2508-6; PB is 47.50: ISBN 0-7883-2509-4. 175p.

Vitamin P Complex - Bioflavonoids: Index of New Information and Guide-Book for Consumers, Reference and Research. May 2002. Cloth, 57.50: 0-83-2524-8; PB is 47.50: ISBN 0-7883-2525-6. 175p.

Vitamin B-T: Carnitine: Index of New Information and Guide-Book for Consumers, Reference and Research. June 2002. Cloth, 57.50; ISBN 0-7883-2526-4; PB is 47.50: ISBN 0-7883-2527-2. 175,

ABBE INDEXES CONNECT YOU TO THE WORLD

LITERATURE AND PUT YOU AT THE BORDER OF

THE UNKNOWN WORLD OF RESEARCH.

BIBLIOGRAPHIC INFORMATION FOR ALL NATIONS

RESEARCH AND PROGRESS FOR ALL MANKIND

NEW REFERNCE BOOKS AND RESEARCH INDEXES

PLANET EARTH IGNORES THE IMPORTANCE OF RESEARCH

Choking and Air-Way Obstructions: Index of New Information for Consumers, Reference and Research. May 202. Cloth, 57.50: ISBN 0-7883-2546-9; PB is 47.50: ISBN 0-7883-2547-7. 175p.

Food Alterations & Contaminations: Index of New Information and Guide-Book for Consumers, Reference and Research. April 2002. Cloth, 57.50: ISBN 0-7883-2550-7; PB is 47.50: ISBN 0-7883-2551-5.

Health Dangers of Free Radical Chemistry: Index of New Information and Guide-book for Consumers, Reference and Research. April 2002. Cloth, 57.50: ISBN 0-7883-2552-3; PB is 47.50: ISBN 0-7883-2553-1. 175p.

Elbow - Its injuries and Cubital Tunnel Syndrome: Index of New Information and Guide-Book for Consumers, Reference and Research. May 2002. Cloth, 57.50: ISBN 0-7883-2554-X; PB is 47.50: ISBN 0-7883-2555-8. 175p.

Neuro-Protective Agents & Therapeutic Uses: Index of New Information and Guide-Book for Consumers, Reference and Research. May 202. Cloth, 57.50: ISBN 0-7883-2566-3; PB is 47.50: ISBN 0-7883- 2567-1. 175p.

LASIK Eye Surgery (Laser in Situ) (Kerato-mileusis): Index of New Information and Guide-Book for Consumers, Reference and Research. February 2002. Cloth, 57.50: ISBN 0-7883-2500-0; PB is 47.50: ISBN 0-2501-9. 175p.

Mis-Conduct and Illegal Behavior in Science & Medicine: Index of New Information and Guide-Book For Consumers, Reference and Research. May 2002. Cloth, 57.50: ISBN 0-7883-2568-X; PB is 47.50: ISBN 0-7883-2569-8. 175p.

Science on Planet Earth -Progress, Comments, Controversy, Editorials and Economics: Index of New Information and Guide-Book for Consumers, Reference and Research. May 2002. Cloth, 57.50: ISBN 0-7883-2406-3; PB is 47.50: ISBN 0-7883-2407-1. 175p.

ABBE INDEXES BRING YOU TO THE UNKNOWN WORLD WHERE YOU CAN VIEW, SEARCH, EXPERIMENT OR TAKE NEW IDEAS FOR MONEY, FAME OR HONOR. TAKE YOUR PICK.

BIBLIOGRAPHIC INFORMATION FOR ALL NATIONS

RESEARCH AND PROGRESS FOR ALL MANKIND

NEW REFERENCE BOOKS AND RESEARCH INDEXES

RICH NATIONS... PERFORM MORE RESEARCH... ...THAN POOR NATIONS

Microbiology of Air: Index of New Information and Guide-book for Consumers, Reference and Research. March 2002. Cloth, 57.50: ISBN 0-7883-2296-6; PB is 47.50: ISBN 0-7883-2297-4. 175p.

Movement Discomfort & Disorders (Dyskinesias): Index of New Information for Consumers, Reference and Research. June 2002. Cloth, 57.50: ISBN 0-7883-2408-X; PB is 47.50: ISBN 0-7883-2409-8. 175p.

Cancer and Chromosome Aberrations: Index of New Information for Consumers, Reference and Research. June 2002. Cloth, 57.50: ISBN 0-7883-2420-9; PB is 47.50: ISBN 0-7883-2421-7. 175p.

Vegetarianism For Family Health & Longevity: Index of New Information for Consumers, Reference and Research. January 2002. Cloth, 57.50: ISBN 0-7883-2422-5; PB is 47.50: ISBN 0-7883-2423-3. 175p.

Life Stress, Distress and Depression in the psychological garden of mental illness and the complex variations in human activities: Index of New Information for Consumers, Reference and Research. May 2002. Cloth, 57.50: ISBN 0-7883-2424-1; PB is 47.50: ISBN 0-7883-2425-X. 175p.

Appetite Disturbances & Disorders - Early behavior and hyperphagia. Index of New Information for Consumers, Reference and Research. May 2002. Cloth, 57.50: ISBN 0-7883-2426-8; PB is 47.50: ISBN 0-7883-2427-6. 175p.

Obesity & Anti-obesity Agents: Index of New Information for Consumers, Reference and Research. March 2002. Cloth, 57.50: ISBN 0-7883-2432-2; PB is 47.50: ISBN 0-7883-2433-0. 175p.

HIV Epidemic Continues in the United States: Index of New Information for Consumers, Reference and Research. January 2002. Cloth, 57.50: ISBN 0-7883-2442-X; PB is 47.50: ISBN 0-7883-2443-8. 175p.

ABBE INDEXES BRING YOU TO THE GOAL LINE BETWEEN KNOWN & UNKNOWN INFORMATION. THERE, YOU CAN MAKE NEW DISCOVERIES FOR HEALTH, MONEY, INVENTION OR ENTERTAINMENT.

BIBLIOGRAPHIC INFORMATION FOR ALL NATIONS

RESEARCH AND PROGRESS FOR ALL MANKIND

NEW REFERENCE BOOKS AND RESEARCH INDEXES

RESEARCH: THE MOST NEGLECTED AREA IN THE ENTIRE WORLD

AIDS & HIV Long term survivors --Analysis and Results: Index of New Information and Guide-Book for Consumers, Reference and Research. January 2002. Cloth, 57.50: ISBN 0-7883-2444-6; PB is ISBN 0-7883- 2445-4. 175p.

Human Anatomy with Over-Use Syndromes and Cumulative Trauma Disorders: Index of New Information and Guide-Book for Consumers, Reference and Research. February 2002. Cloth 57.50: ISBN 0-7883-2446-2; PB is 47.50: ISBN 0-7883-2447-0. 175p.

Biogenesis of Life- In fact, theory and controversy: Index of New Information and Guide-Book for Consumers, Reference and Research. April 2002. Cloth, 57.50: ISBN 0-7883-2458-6; PB is 47.50: ISBN 0-7883-2459-4. 175p.

Evolution & The Origin of Life: Index of New Information and Guide-Book for Consumers, Reference and Research. April 2002. Cloth, 57.50: ISBN 0-7883-2476-4; PB is 47.50: ISBN 0-7883-2477-2. 175p.

Over-weight, Over-eating, obesity and morbidity in America: Index of New Information and Guide-Book for Consumers, Reference and Research. April 2002. Cloth, 57.50: ISBN 0-7883-2490-X; PB is 47.50: ISBN 0-7883- 2491-8. 175p.

Sleep -Deficiency, Deprivations, Disturbances and Disorders: Index of New Information and Guide-Book for Consumers, Reference and Research. February 2002. Cloth, 57.50: ISBN 0-7883-2494-2; PB is 47.50: ISBN 0-7883- 2495-0. 175p.

African-Americans -Analysis, Behavior, Progress and Results: Index of New Information and Guide-Book for Consumers, Reference and Research. February 2002. Cloth 57.50: ISBN 0-7883-1484-X; PB is 47.50: ISBN 0-7883- 1495-5. 175p.

Humor, Mirth & Mischief at Life and Philosophy: Snappy lines for Home, Office and parties or for everyday laughs. Cloth, 34.95: ISBN 0-7883-1058-5; PB is 24.95: ISBN 0-7883-1059-3. 150p.

ABBE INDEXES INTRODUCE YOU TO THE MOST EXCITING "GAME" IN THE WORLD:

NEW RESEARCH FOR WORLD DEVELOPMENT

BIBLIOGRAPHIC INFORMATION FOR ALL NATIONS

RESEARCH AND PROGRESS FOR ALL MANKIND

NEW REFERENCE BOOKS AND RESEARCH INDXES

RESEARCH IS OUR BEST SALVATION AGAINST DISEASE & FILTH

Anger and Rage --Analysis and Conclusions of Life of Modern Times: Index of New Information and Guide-Book for Consumers, Reference & Research. February 2002. Cloth, 57.50: ISBN 0-7883-2342-3 PB is 47.50: ISBN 0-7883-2343-1.180p.

Cancer Epidemics Are World-Wide and Affecting All Parts of the Human Body: Index of New Information and Guide-Book for Consumers, Reference and Research. March 2002. Cloth, 67.50: ISBN 0-7883-2404-7; PB is 57.50: ISBN 0-7883-2405-5. 175p.

Coffee –America's Favorite All-Day Beverage and Relaxation Drink: Index of New Information and Guide-Book for Consumers, Reference and Research. May 2002. Cloth 57.57: ISBN 0-7883-2594-9; Pb is 47.50: ISBN 0-7883-2595-7. 180P.

American Attitudes: U.S. Register A to Z: Index and Analysis of New Information and Guide-Book for Consumers, Reference and Research. 5 Volumes: Cloth is $ 425.00; ISBN for 5 volumes is 0-7883-2876-X; Pb of 5 volumes is $ 375.00; ISBN 0-7883-2877-8.
*Each volume: Cloth is $ 85.00 each; Pb is $ 75.00 each.

BIOTERRORISM–A Biological and Medical Bibliography of 1200 Citations for Reference, Research and Preparedness. June 2002. Cloth is $85.50 ISBN 0-7883-2707-0; PB is $ 75.50, ISBN 0-7883-2708-9. 275p.

FETAL ALCOHOL SYNDROME –THE MAN-MADE DISEASE FOR BABIES AND CHILDREN: INDEX OF NEW INFORMATION. 3rd Edition. September 2002. Cloth is $ 57.50, ISBN 0-7883-2734-8; Pb is 47.50, ISBN 0-7883-2735-6.160p.

HELSINKI DECLARATION: BIOETHICAL ISSUES, CLINICAL RIGHTS OF HUMANS, PRINCIPLES OF RESEARCH ON HUMANS AND NATURE OF HUMAN EXPERIMENTATION. June 2002. Cloth is 57.50, ISBN 0-7883-2830-1; Pb is 47.50, ISBN 0-7883-2831-X.

HOT FLASHES: Index of New Information and Guide-Book for Consumers, Reference and Research. June 2002. Cloth $ 57.50, ISBN 0-7883-2730-5; Pb is 47.50, ISBN 0-7883-2731-3.160p.

WEST NILE FEVER–Outbreaks and Conditions in the U.S. and Elsewhere: Index of New Information and Guide-Book for Reference, Research & Clinical Uses. September 2002. Cloth $ 57.50, ISBN 0-7883-2742-9; PB 47.50 ISBN 0-7883-2743-7.

ABBE INDEXES MAKE WORLD PROGRESS FOR ALL

BIBLIOGRAPHIC INFORMATION FOR ALL NATIONS

RESEARCH AND PROGRESS FOR ALL MANKIND

NEW REFERENCE BOOKS AND RESEARCH INDEXES

HOW CAN ANYONE IMPROVE THE HEALTH OF ALL PEOPLE? BY ONE SIMPLE MANEUVER: TAKE THE POLITICS OUT OF RESEARCH PROJECTS !

CANCER ENCYCLOPEDIA --Collections of Anti-Cancer and Anti-Carcinogenic Agents, chemicals, drugs and substances: Index of New Information and Guide-Book for Consumers, Reference and Research. January 2002. Volumes are available as a set or as separate volumes in Hardcover or Paperback. Author: Dr. John C. Bartone.

20 Volume set. Hardcover: 0-7883-2650-3: $ 1310.00. Approx 3600+ pages.
(Paperback listings follow on the next page)

Volume 1 (1969-1979) Cloth, 65.50: ISBN 0-7883-2652-X. 180p.
Volume 2 (1980-1985) Cloth, 65.50: ISBN 0-7883-2654-6. 180p.
Volume 3 (1986-1988) Cloth, 65.50: ISBn 0-7883-2656-2. 180p.
Volume 4 (1989-1991) Cloth, 65.50: ISBN 0-7883-2658-9. 180p.
Volume 5 (1992)   Cloth, 65.50: ISBN 0-7883-2660-0. 180p.
Volume 6 (1993)   Cloth, 65.50: ISBN 0-7883-2662-7. 180p.
Volume 7 (1994)   Cloth, 65.50: ISBN 0-7883-2664-3. 180p.
Volume 8 (1995A)   Cloth, 65.50: ISBN 0-7883-2666-X. 180p.
Volume 9 (1995B)   Cloth, 65-50: ISBN 0-7883-2668-6. 180p.
Volume 10 (1996A)   Cloth, 65-50: ISBN 0-7883-2670-8. 180p.
Volume 11 (1996B)   Cloth, 65.50: ISBN 0-7883-2672-4. 180p.
Volume 12 (1997A)   Cloth, 65.50: ISBN 0-7883-2674-0. 180p.
Volume 13 (1997B)   Cloth, 65.50: ISBN 0-7883-2676-7. 180p.
Volume 14 (1998A)   Cloth, 65.50: ISBN 0-7883-2678-3. 180p.
Volume 15 (1998B)   Cloth, 65.50: ISBN 0-7883-2680-5. 180p.
Volume 16 (1999A)   Cloth, 65.50: ISBN 0-7883-2682-1. 180p.
Volume 17 (1999B)   Cloth, 65.50: ISBN 0-7883-2684-8. 180p.
Volume 18 (2000A)   Cloth, 65.50: ISBN 0-7883-2686-4. 180p.
Volume 19 (2000B)   Cloth, 65.50: ISBN 0-7883-2688-0. 180p.
Volume 20 (2000C)   Cloth, 65.50: ISBN 0-7883-2690-2. 180p.
20 Volume Set: Hardcover: 0-7883-2650-3: $ 1310.00 Approx 3600+ pages.
Paperback volumes, price and ISBN follow on the next page.

Collective Bargining, Labor Unions and Negotiations: Index of New Information for Analysis, Reference and Research. May 2002. Cloth $ 57.50, ISBN 0-7883-2640-6; Pb is $ 47.50, ISBN 0-7883-2641-4. 180p.

MANDATORY TESTING OF SUBSTANCE ABUSE: INDEX OF NEW INFORMATION AND GUIDE-BOOK FOR REFERENCE AND RESEARCH. 2nd Edition Cloth Cloth $65.00, ISBN 0-7883-2782-6; Pb is $47.50, ISBN 0-7883-2783-6.

POLICE –Health, Risks, Shift Work, Attitudes and Brutality Force: Index of New information. 2nd Revision, New. Cloth $61.00, ISBN is 0-7884-2890-5; PB is $51.00, ISBN is 0-7883-2891-3.180p.

BIBLIOGRAPHIC INFORMATION FOR ALL NATIONS

RESEARCH AND PROGRESS FOR ALL MANKIND

NEW REFERENCE BOOKS AND RESEARCH INDEXES

WORLD COMMERCIALISM IS INVOLVED IN WORLD-WIDE CANCER EPIDEMICS

CANCER ENCYCLOPEDIA -Collections of Anti-Cancer & Anti-Carcinogenic Agents, Chemicals, Drugs and Substances: Index of New Information and Guide-Book for Consumers, Reference and Research. January 2002. Approx 3600 pages. Dr. John C. Bartone.

PAPERBACK VOLUMES: AVAILABLE AS SET OR AS INDIVIDUAL VOLUMES:
**Publication Date: January 2002.
20 Volume set: Paperback: ISBN 0-7883-2651-1: $ 1110.00; Approx 3600 pages.

Volume   1 (1966-1979) Paperback, 55.50: ISBN 0-7883-2653-8. 180p.
Volume   2 (1980-1985) Paperback, 55.50: ISBN 0-7883-2655-4. 180p.
Volume   3 (1986-1988) Paperback, 55.50: ISBN 0-7883-2657-0. 180p.
Volume   4 (1989-1991) Paperback, 55.50: ISBN 0-7883-2659-7. 180p.
Volume   5 (1992)   Paperback, 55.50: ISBN 0-7883-2661-9. 180p.
Volume   6 (1993)   Paperback, 55.50: ISBN 0-7883-2663-5. 180p.
Volume   7 (1994)   Paperback, 55.50: ISBN 0-7883-2665-1. 180p.
Volume   8 (1995A)   Paperback, 55.50: ISBN 0-7883-2667-8. 180p.
Volume   9 (1885B)   Paperback, 55.50: ISBN 0-7885-2669-4. 180p.
Volume 10 (1996A)   Paperback, 55.50: ISBN 0-7883-2671-6. 180p.
Volume 11 (1996B)   Paperback, 55.50: ISBN 0-7883-2673-2. 180p.
Volume 12 (1997A)   Paperback, 55.50: ISBN 0-7883-2675-9. 180p.
Volume 13 (1997B)   Paperback, 55.50: ISBN 0-7883-2677-5. 180p.
Volume 14 (1998A)   Paperback, 55.50: ISBN 0-7883-2679-1. 180p.
Volume 15 (1998B)   Paperback, 55.50: ISBN 0-7883-2681-3. 180p.
Volume 16 (1999A)   Paperback, 55.50: ISBN 0-7883-2683-X. 180p.
Volume 17 (1999B)   Paperback, 55.50: ISBN 0-7883-2685-6. 180p.
Volume 18 (2000A)   Paperback, 55.50: ISBN 0-7883-2687-2. 180p.
Volume 19 (2000B)   Paperback, 55.50: ISBN 0-7883-2689-9. 180p.
Volume 20 (2000C)   Paperback, 55.50: ISBN 0-7883-2691-0. 180p.

Pneumonia —Medical Subject Analysis, Reference and Research Guide-Book. January 2002. Cloth $57.50, ISBN 0-7883-2804-2; Pb is $47.50, ISBN 0-7883-2805-0. 180p.

Pollutant Materials —Index of New Information and Guide-Book for Consumers, Reference & Research. January 2002. Cloth $57.50, ISBN 0-7883-2572-8; Pb is $47.50, ISBN 0-7883-2573-4.

NEURO-TOXINS —Index of New Information and Research Reference Bible. April 2001. Cloth $57.50, ISBN 0-7883-2452-7; PB is 47.50, ISBN 0-7883-2453-5. 180p.

ABBE INDEXES HELP EXPAND YOUR EXPERTISE

BIBLIOGRAPHIC INFORMATION FOR ALL NATIONS

RESEARCH AND PROGRESS FOR ALL MANKIND

NEW REFERENCE BOOKS AND RESEARCH INDEXES

NEGLECT OF RESEARCH PROGRESS INCREASES CRIME, DISEASE & POVERTY

EMBRYO RESEARCH IN TODAY'S WORLD: Index of New Information and Guide-Book for Consumers, Reference and Research. January 2002. Cloth is $57.50, ISBN 0-7883-2700-3; PB is $47.50, ISBN 0-7883-2701-1. Dr. Joy W. Rader. 180p.

ORGAN DONATIONS OF HUMANS: index of New Information and Guide-Book for Consumers, Reference and Research. January 2002. Cloth is 57.50, ISBN 0-7883-2574-4; Pb is $47.50, ISBN 0-7883-2575-2. 180p.

SEX, DYSFUNCTIONS AND PARAPHILIAS: Index of New Information and Guide-Book for Consumers, Reference and Research. Jan 2002. Cloth is $57.50 ISBN 0-7883-2578-7; PB is $47.50, ISBN 0-7883-2579-5. 180p.

SOCCER –REPORT FOR ATHLETES, COACHES AND CONSUMERS; Index of New Information and Guide-Book for Consumers, Reference and Research. January 2002. Cloth is $57.50, ISBN 0-7883-2582-5; Pb is $47.50, ISBN 0-7883-2583-3. 180p.

COMPUTER NETWORKS IN THE HEALTH PROFESSIONS; Index of New Information and Guide-Book for Consumers, Reference and Research. January 2002. Cloth $57.50, ISBN 0-7883-2596-5; Pb is 47.50, ISBN 0-7883-2597-3. 180p.

CHEMICAL WARFARE; Index of New information and Guide-Book for Consumers, Reference and Research. January 2002. Cloth 57.50; ISBN 0-7883-2598-1; Pb is $47.50, ISBN 0-7883-2599-X.

INFANT FOOD: Index of New Information and Guide-Book for Consumers, Reference and Research. February 2002. Cloth $57.50, ISBN 0-7883-2624-4; Pb is $47.50, ISBN 0-7883-2625-2.

SEX AND ORGASM; index of New Information and Guide-Book for Consumers, Reference and Research. February 2002. Cloth $57.50, ISBN 0-7883-2748-8; Pb is $47.50, ISBN 0-7883-2749-6.

COMPUTERS –USE AND DEVELOPMENT FOR HEALTH SCIENTISTS; Index of New Information and Guide-Book for Consumers, Reference and Research. February 2002. Cloth $57.50, ISBN 0-7883-2738-0; Pb is 47.50, ISBN 0-7883-2739-9. 180p.

Breast CANCER; Index of New Information and Guide-Book for Consumers, Reference and Research. January 2002. Cloth $57.50, ISBN 0-7883-2606-6; Pb is $47.50, ISBN 0-7883-2607-4.

ABBE INDEXES TAKE YOU TO WORLD-FAMOUS RESEARCH PLAYGROUNDS

BIBLIOGRAPHIC INFORMATION FOR ALL NATIONS
RESEARCH AND PROGRESS FOR ALL MANKIND
NEW REFERENCE BOOKS AND RESEARCH INDEXES

RICH NATIONS PROFIT THE MOST FROM ALL FORMS OF RESEARCH

BIOLOGY OF WARFARE: Index of New Information and Guide-Book for Consumers, Reference and Research. January 2002. Cloth $57.50, ISBN 0-7883-2638-4; Pb is $47.50, ISBN 0-7883-2639-2.

POLLUTANT MATERIALS: Index of New Information and Guide-Book for Consumers, Reference and Research. January 2002. Cloth $57.50, ISBN 0-7883-2572-8; Pb is 47.50, ISBN 0-7883-2573-4. 180p.

WESCHSLER SCALES; Index of New Information and Guide-Book for Consumers, Reference and Research. January 2002. Cloth $57.50, ISBN 0-7883-2718-6; Pb is $47.50, ISBN 0-7883-2719-4. 180p.

BETA-CAROTENE: Index of New Information and Guide-Book for Consumers, Reference and Research. January 2002. Cloth $57.50, ISBN 0-7883-2590-6; Pb is $47.50, ISBN 0-7883=2591-4. 180p.

Menstruation Disturbances: Index of New Information and Guide-Book for Consumers, Reference and Research. March 2002. Cloth, 57.50:ISBN 0-7883-2528-0; PB is ISBN 0-7883-2529-9. 175p.

**ABBE INDEXES HELP YOU TO MEET SOME OF THE MOST FAMOUS, PRODUCTIVE AND FRIENDLY PHYSICIANS AND SCIENTISTS OF THIS WORLD.

"....BE AN EXPERT WITH ABBE INDEXES...."

THE IMPORTANCE OF REFERENCE & INDEX BOOKS

REFERENCE BOOKS, NEW OR OLD, NEVER DIE OR BECOME OBSOLETE FOR THEY TELL OF THE PROGRESS OF THE PRESENT ERA, YIELD MANY LANDMARKS OF THE PAST AND SERVE AS WISE GUIDE-POSTS TO THE FUTURE OF ALL MANKIND.

Dr. John C. Bartone
American Scientist
1946

'BE AN EXPERT WITH ABBE INDEXES..."

NEW REFERENCE BOOKS
AND
RESEARCH INDEXES

OUR CONCERN IS YOUR HEALTH -AND THAT OF THE WORLD!

- GOOD HEALTH IS OUR GREATEST WEALTH -

WHAT ARE WE WITHOUT GOOD HEALTH?

ALL THESE BOOKS CONTAIN THE LATEST INFORMATION.

THESE BOOKS HAVE KNOWLEDGE BEYOND MODERN TEXTBOOKS FOR YOUR PERSONAL AND PROFESSIONAL WELFARE

PROMOTE, ENHANCE AND EXPAND YOUR EXPERTISE BY A QUICK VISIT TO OUR CATALOG IN BOWKER'S "BOOKS IN PRINT".

GREAT IMPROVEMENTS ARE MADE SIMPLE: GET RESEARCH !!

COMPLETE TITLES ARE LISTED IN "BOOKS IN PRINT".

EACH PAGE OFFERS A SIMPLE STATEMENT FOR THE FUTURE OF YOUR WELL-BEING, FOR THE NATION AND THE WORLD.

MANKIND HAS YET TO LEARN THAT RESEARCH IS THE BEST SOLUTION FOR ANY PROBLEM.

ANY BOOKSTORE, DISTRIBUTOR OR WHOLESALER CAN ORDER THESE BOOKS FOR YOU VERY FAST.

*All titles are shortened to save you time and energy. Full information is always available in BOOKS IN PRINT. All titles available in hardcover or paperback.

- ABORTION: INDEX
- ABORTION & RU486: INDEX
- ABSENTEEISM, WORK LOSS & ILLNESS: INDEX
- ABSTRACTING & INDEXING: INDEX
- ACCIDENT PREVENTION & INJURY CONTROL: INDEX
- ACCIDENTS IN OCCUPATIONS & INDUSTRY: INDEX
- ACCIDENTS OF ALL TYPES & FORMS: INDEX

REFERENCE BOOKS CONTAIN NEW, FRESH AND EXCITING RESEARCH SUGGESTIONS.

>>>>>BE AN EXPERT WITH ABBE INDEXES >>>>>

New Research gives all children better health-care.

NEW REFERENCE BOOKS & RESEARCH INDEXES

WITHOUT RESEARCH OUR LIFE-SPAN WOULD BE LESS THAN 40 YEARS!

ACETAMINOPHEN: INDEX
ETHYLENE: INDEX
ACIDOSIS: INDEX
ACUPUNCTURE: INDEX
ACYCLOVIR: INDEX
ADOLESCENT BEHAVIOR: INDEX
ADOLESCENT PSYCHOLOGY: INDEX
ADVERSE EFFECTS OF AIR POLLUTANTS: INDEX
ADVERSE EFFECTS OF ASPIRIN: INDEX
ADVERSE EFFECTS OF LITHIUM: INDEX

ADVERSE EFFECTS OF RADIOTHERAPY: INDEX
ADVERTISING & MEDICINE: GUIDEBOOK INDEX
AEROSPACE MEDICINE: INDEX
AGED & THE ELDERLY: INDEX
AGGRESSION: INDEX
AIR ANALYSIS FOR HEALTH & DANGERS AT HOME:
AIR POLLUTANTS: INDEX
AIR POLLUTION FUNGUS & MOLDS IN HOMES, ET
AIRCRAFTS & AIR TRANSPORT IN COMMERCE & MED:

ALCOHOL DRINKING: INDEX
ALKALOSIS: INDEX
ALLERGY & IMMUNOLOGY: INDEX
ALUMINUM: INDEX
ALZHEIMER'S DISEASE: INDEX
AMBULATORY CARE: INDEX
ANATOMY & HEALTH SCIENCE: INDEX
ANIMAL BEHAVIOR: INDEX
ANIMAL COMMUNICATIONS: INDEX
ANIMAL HUSBANDRY: INDEX

ANIMAL PHYSIOLOGY: INDEX
ANIMAL SOCIAL BEHAVIOR: INDEX
ANIMAL TESTING ALTERNATIVES
ANIMAL WELFARE: INDEX
ANIMALS IN MEDICINE & RESEARCH
ANIMALS IN WILDLIFE: INDEX
ANTHROPOLOGY OF MINORITY GROUPS
ANTI-OXIDANTS: INDEX
ANTI-OXIDANTS: EFFECTS ON LONGEVITY

NEW REFERENCE BOOKS & RESEARCH INDEXES

NEW RESEARCH LEADS TO PROGRESS
AND
HEALTH IMPROVEMENTS FOR YOU....

ANTI-OXIDANTS & TOXICITY RESEARCH
ANTIBIOTICS & ADVERSE EFFECTS
ANXIETY -PREVENTION & CONTROL
ANXIETY DISORDERS
APTITUDE TESTS
ARM INJURIES

ARTIFICIAL INTELLIGENCE
ASBESTOS & ASBESTOSIS
ASPIRIN -REPORTS OF HARMFUL EFFECTS
ATHEROSCLEROSIS: INDEX OF REVIEWS
ATHEROSCLEROSIS & ATHERECTOMY

ATHLETIC INJURIES: GUIDEBOOK
ATTEMPTED SUICIDE: GUIDEBOOK
ATTITUDE & ATTITUDES: INDEX
ATTITUDES TO DEATH & DYING
AUDIO-VISUAL AIDS IN HEALTH BIOLOGY
AUTOMATIC DATA TECHNOLOGY
AUTOMATION & AUTOANALYSIS IN MED
AUTO ACCIDENTS, PREVENTION & CONTROL
AUTO EXHAUST IN HEALTH & DISEASE

BACK PAIN & SPINAL PROBLEMS
BACTERIA: INDEX OF REVIEWS
BACTERIAL INFECTIONS
BARTONE'S GUIDEBOOK TO BIOL WARFARE
BARTONELLA INFECTIONS
BEHAVIOR & MOTIVATION
BEHAVIOR IN MIND & BODY BY CHOICE
BEHAVIORAL SCIENCES
BENZENE

BETA-CAROTENE & CAROTENOIDS
BEVERAGES, DRINKS & JUICES
BIBLE QUOTATIONS MADE HUMOROUS
BIBLES: INDEX OF MODERN INFORMATION
BIBLIOGRAPHY & DOCUMENTATION IN HEALTH
BIBLIOGRAPHY PUBLICATIONS
BIO-ETHICS: INDEX
BIOLOGICAL PRODUCTS & ACTIONS
BIOLOGY IN THE HEALTH SCIENCES

NEW REFERENCE BOOKS & RESEARCH INDEXES

REFERENCE BOOKS & INDEXES ARE PIONEERS
AND LEAD YOU
INTO NEW UNKNOWN VISTAS
FOR GREATER WEALTH,
WISDOM AND HEALTH

BIOLOGY OF ALLIGATORS & CROCODILES
BIOLOGY OF COCKROACHES: INDEX
BIOLOGY OF FLEAS: INDEX
BIOLOGY OF SURVIVAL: HUMAN, ANIMAL LIFE
BIOMEDICAL ENGINEERING
BIORHYTHMS, BIOLOGICAL CLOCKS & PERIODICITY
BIOSENSORS & TECHNICAL MED
BIOTECHNOLOGY
BIRTH INJURIES

BLACKS & THE NEGROID RACE
BLACKS & THEIR BIO-MEDICAL HISTORY
BLACKS--STATUS & PROGRESS
BLACKS--THEIR PSYCHOLOGY & BEHAVIOR

BLINDNESS
BLOOD PRESSURE & DRUG EFFECTS
BLOOD SUBSTITUTES & THER USES
BRAIN INJURIES
BRAIN METABOLIC DISEASES
BREAST CANCERS, CHEMICALLY INDUCED
BREATH TESTS IN HEALTH, SCIENCE & MEDICINE
BUFOTENIN (DIMETHYLSEROTONIN)
BURNS-THERAPY & PSYCHOLOGY

BUTTER--ANALYSIS, COMPOSITION, USES, FLAVOR
CAESARIAN SECTION & BIRTH FACTORS
CAFFEINE: INDEX

CANCER & CARCINOGENS IN HOME, WORK, ET
CANCER AND ITS CAUSES
CANCER & IT PSYCHOLOGICAL INFLUENCES
CANCER & PRECANCEROUS CONDITIONS
CANCER--RESEARCH ON CAUSES
CANCER PREVENTION & CONTROL
CANCER THERAPY--METHODS, TREATMENT, ET
CANCER VARIATIONS & MORTALITY
CANCERS--BY EXPERIMENTS, CHEM PRODUCTS
CANCERS PRODUCED BY RADIATION
CANNABIS (MARIJUANA)

CARCINOGENS

NEW REFERENCE BOOKS & RESEARCH INDEXES

NEW INFORMATION PROLONGS LIFE -
AND
SOMETIMES HAPPINESS TOO!

CARDIOPULMONARY BYPASS
CARPAL TUNNEL SYNDROME-CAUSES, TREATMENT
CAT DISEASES & VET MED
CELL NEOPLASTIC TRANSFORMATION
CEREALS, GRAIN, MALT & MILLET
CHARITIES, GOOD WILL & DIVINE GIVING

CHEMICAL INDUCTION, NEW TUMORS, CANCER
CHILD ABUSE: REFERENCE GUIDE & INDEX
CHILD ABUSE II: REFERENCE GUIDE & INDEX
CHILD PLAY & PLAYTHINGS: INDEX
CHILD WELFARE & FOSTER HOME CARE
CHILDREN'S DAILY VERSES FOR FUN & PLAY
CHIN AND MANDIBLE
CHIROPRACTIC PRACTICE-METHODS, TRENDS
CHRISTIANITY: INDEX OF MODERN INFO
CHROMIUM IN HEALTH, DISEASE & INDUSTRY

CIRCUMCISION: PROS AND
CIVIL DEFENSE IN WAR & PEACE
CIVIL RIGHTS
CLOTHING, HEALTH, HAZARD, STYLES, IMAGE PSYC
COCAINE & ITS DAMAGING INFLUENCES
COMMUNICABLE DISEASES
COMMUNICATION-PERSUASIVE, MASTER-MIND, PROPAGANDA
COMMUNICATION IN MED & PSYCHOLOGY
COMMUNISM: INDEX

COMPETITIVE BEHAVIOR

COMPUTER ADVANCEMENTS IN HEALTH SCIENCE
COMPUTER ASSISTED INSTRUCTION IN HS
COMPUTER COMMUNICATION NETWORKS
COMPUTER SCIEBCE & INFORMATICS IN MEDICINE
COMPUTER SCIENCE IN HEALTH SCIENCE
COMPUTER ASSISTED DIAGNOSIS
COMPUTER ASSISTED INSTRUCTION & EDUCATION
CONSERVATION

CONSUMER & PATIENT SATISFACTION
CONSUMER & PUBLIC DISCLOSURE OF CONDOMS
CONSUMER ATTITUDES & WISH OF HEALTH CARE

NEW REFERENCE BOOKS & RESEARCH INDEXES

AUTHORS (SCIENTISTS) PRODUCE RESEARCH
AND
NEW PRODUCTS
FOR BETTER LIFE, NOW AND FUTURE LIVING

CONSUMER CAR CARE FOR WISE, POOR & HELPLESS
CONSUMER INDEX BOOK: COCAINE & DANGER
CONSUMER INDEX: HAZARD SUBSTANCE IN YOUR LIFE
CONSUMER INDEX ABOUT HIV, AIDS & TREATMENTS
CONSUMER INDEX ABOUT INFORMED CONSENT
CONSUMERS' ATTITUDES TO HEALTH CARE
CONSUMER'S' INDEX ABOUT DIAGNOSTIC ERRORS
CONSUMER'S' DATA BOOK OF ACTIVITIES, INVESTIG, ORG

CONSUMERS' INDEX: WHAT'S GOING ON IN LIFE, ET
CONSUMERS' INDEX ABOUT ABORTION, TODAY'S WORLD
CONSUMERS' INDEX ABOUT ADOLESCENT BEHAVIOR
CONSUMERS' INDEX ABOUT AUTO ACCIDENTS
CONSUMERS' INDEX ABOUT CIVIL RIGHTS

CONSUMERS' INDEX ABOUT COSMETICS GOOD & BAD
CONSUMERS' INDEX ABOUT CRIME PREVENTION
CONSUMERS' INDEX ABOUT CRIME TODAY IN U.S.A.
CONSUMERS' INDEX ABOUT EXERCISE
CONSUMER'S INDEX ABOUT FOOD, DIET & CANCER
CONSUMERS' INDEX ABOUT HUMAN RIGHTS

CONSUMERS' INDEX ABOUT HYPNOSIS
CONSUMERS' INDEX ABOUT ILLNESS & DISEASE BY JOBS
CONSUMERS' INDEX ABOUT JUVENILE DELINQUENCY
CONSUMERS' INDEX LOVE AND LIBIDO

CONSUMERS' INDEX ABOUT MAGIC & SUPERSTITIONS
CONSUMERS' INDEX ABOUT MARRIAGE
CONSUMERS' INDEX ABOUT MASSAGE
CONSUMERS' INDEX ABOUT NUTRITION
CONSUMERS' INDEX ABOUT RELAXATION & METHODS

CONSUMERS' INDEX ABOUT RIGHTS TO MED TREATMENT
CONSUMERS' INDEX ABOUT SEX & BISEXUALITY
CONSUMERS' INDEX ABOUT SEX COUNSELING & DISEASE
CONSUMERS' INDEX ABOUT SPORTS

CONSUMERS' INDEX ABOUT STRESS, DISTRESS & TRMT
CONSUMERS' INDEX ABOUT HEALTH BENEFITS OF GARLIC
CONSUMERS' INDEX ABOUT .....DEATH

NEW REFERENCE BOOKS & RESEARCH INDEXES

NATIONS OR PEOPLE WITHOUT RESEARCH PROGRESS BECOME EASY VICTIMS OF TIME, ROT AND SICK HEALTH

CONSUMERS' INDEX ABOUT MEDICAL MALPRACTICE
CONSUMERS' RIGHTS AS ARMED CITIZENS
CONSUMERS' INDEX: WHAT'S GOING ON IN LIFE, ET
CONSUMERS' INDEX ABOUT ABORTION

CONTRACEPTION & FAMILY PLANNING
CORONARY DISEASE

COSMETICS & BEAUTY CULTURE
COSMETICS & HEALTH
COTTON --IN HEALTH, WORK & INDUSTRY
COUNSELING-GUIDE, INTERVENTION, SKILLS, MGT, SEX

CRIME
CRIME & CRIMINAL NOTIONS
CRIME & CRIMINAL PSYCHOLOGY

CRIME AND RIOT CONTROL
CRIME ANALYSIS-WITH MED, FORENSIC, POLITICS
CRIME PREVENTION AND CONTROL
CRIME RESEARCH INDEX

CRIMINAL PSYCHOLOGY
CRISIS INTERVENTION
CURRICULUMS IN HEALTH SCIENCES
CYSTIC FIBROSIS
DEATH
DEATH & POST CHANGES, NORM & MYSTERIOUS
DECISION MAKING IN HEALTH
DELIVERY OF HEALTH CARE & INTL MED
DENTAL CARE & HEALTH FACTORS

DENTAL PRACTICE & RESEARCH
DENTISTRY IN INDUSTRY
DENTISTRY, PATIENTS & DENTISTS

DEODORANTS
DEPRESSION
DEVELOPING COUNTRIES
DIAGNOSIS
DIAGNOSIS & COMPUTERS

NEW REFERENCE BOOKS & RESEARCH INDEXES.

RESEARCH PATHWAYS ARE SECRET ROADS TO DRIVE TO UTOPIA FOR EVERYONE.

DIAGNOSIS OF DEPRESSIVE DISORDERS
DIAGNOSIS OF MENTAL DISORDERS

DIAGNOSTIC ERRORS IN MEDICINE
DIAGNOSTIC TESTS

DIET -IN LIFE, FOOD, OLD AGE & RESEARCH
DIET -INVESTIGATIONS, RESEARCH, RESULTS
DIETARY FIBER

DIETARY FIBER, CALORIES AND CANCER

DIETARY MINERALS & DANGEROUS INFLUENCE

DIETHEL SULFOXIDE (DMSO)

DIOXINS & AGENT ORANGE

DIRECTORIES, ASSOCIATIONS, SOCIETIES
DIRECTORY, NEW REVIEWS: ALCOHOLISM
DIRECTORY, REVIEWS, AMBULATORY SURGERY
DIRECTORY, REVIEWS, ANTI-CANCER AGENTS
DIRECTORY, REVIEWS OF ANTIBIOTICS
DIRECTORY, REVIEWS OF ANTIGENS OF CANCER
DIRECTORY, REVIEWS OF BIOPSY
DIRECTORY, REVIEWS OF CARCINOGENS

DIRECTORY, REVIEWS, CELL MEMBRANES
DIRECTORY, REVIEWS: CERVIX NEOPLASMS
DIRECTORY, REVIEWS OF COENZYMES
DIRECTORY, REVIEWS OF CONTRACEPTION

DIRECTORY, REVIEWS OF CYSTIC FIBROSIS
DIRECTORY, REVIEWS OF DIABETES MELLITUS

DIRECTORY, REVIEWS OF DIETS

DIRECTORY, REVIEWS OF DOMESTIC ANIMALS
DIRECTORY, REVIEWS OF ECOLOGY
DIRECTORY, REVIEWS OF HOMEOSTASIS
DIRECTORY, REVIEWS: IMMUNOGLOBULINS
DIRECTORY, REVIEWS OF IMMUNOTHERAPY

DIRECTORY, REVIEWS OF INTELLIGENCE

NEW REFERENCE BOOKS & RESEARCH INDEXES

RESEARCH IS THE BEATING HEART - AND BLOOD- OF PROGRESS AGAINST ALL FORMS OF DECAY.

DIR ECTORY, REVIEWS OF LEUKOCYTES
DIRECTORY, REVIEWS OF MALARIA
DIRECTORY, REVIEWS OF MENTAL DISORDERS
DIRECTORY, REVIEWS OF MINERAL OIL
DIRECTORY, REVIEWS, NEUROTRANS RECEPT
DIRECTORY, REVIEWS OF PHAGOCYTES
DIRECTORY, REVIEWS OF PHYLOGENY
DIRECTORY, REVIEWS, POST-SURGERY COMPLICATIONS
DIRECTORY, REVIEWS: RHEUMATIC DISEASES
DIRECTORY, REVIEWS, SUDDEN CARDIAC DEATHS

DIRECTORY, REVIEWS: TUMOR NECROSIS FACTOR
DIRECTORY, REVIEWS OF XENOBIOTICS
DISABILITY EVALUATION
DISASTERS & DISASTER PLANNING
DISEASE SUSCEPTIBILITY
DISINFECTION & STERILIZATION

DIVORCE & DIVORCE FACTORS
DNA & RECOMBINANTS

DNA FINGER-PRINTING
DOG DISEASES

DREAMS

DRUG ADDICTION, SUBSTANCE ABUSE & DEPENDENCE
DRUG EFFECTS ON MEMORY
DRUG EFFECTS ON MENTAL PROCESSES
DRUG EFFECTS ON THE FETUS
DRUG THERAPY FACTORS & ADVERSE EFFECTS
DRUG THERAPY IN HEALTH, MED & DISEASE
DRUG WITHDRAWAL SYMPTOMS
DRUGS IN ALL PHASES OF LIFE & MED

DRUGS & PSYCHOLOGICAL EFFECT ON BEHAV
DUST & PNEUMOCONIOSIS
DYSLEXIA
EDEMA RESEARCH

EDUCATION & ITS MEASUREMENT

NEW REFERENCE BOOKS & RESEARCH INDEXES

MUCH GRADUATE RESEARCH OF STUDENTS IS NEVER PUBLISHED AND MADE AVAILABLE TO HELP WORLD PROGRESS: WHY NOT, AND WHO IS AT FAULT?

EDUCATIONAL MEASUREMENT
EFFICIENCY & PERFORMANCE
ELECTRIC INJURIES INCLUDING LIGHTNING
ELECTRONIC MAIL & OFFICE AUTOMATION

ELECTRONICS IN HEALTH SCIENCES
EMOTIONS AND MOODS

EMPLOYMENT, WORK & HEALTH
ENDOCRINOLOGY
ENERGY-GENERATING RESOURCES
EPILEPSY
EPILEPSY: NEW REVIEWS
ESTROGEN DEFICIENCY & DEPRIVATION
ESTROGENS

EUGENICS
EUTHANASIA

EVOLUTION & LIFE SCIENCES

EXERCISE BY WALKING
EXERCISE TESTS & SPORTS MEDICINE
EXERCISE THERAPY
EXERTION
EXPERT TESTIMONY IN MED, LAW, ETC
EYE INJURIES

FACIAL EXPRESSIONS, ANATOMY, ANALYSIS
FACIAL INJURIES I
FAMILY PRACTICE

FAMILY THERAPY
FEAR AND PANIC
FEARS AND PHOBIAS
FEMALE GENITAL DISEASES
FETAL DEVELOPMENT
FETAL MONITORING
FIBER OPTICS
FINGER INJURIES

FIREARMS & GUNSHOT WOUNDS

NEW REFERENCE BOOKS & RESEARCH INDEXES

TO INNOVATE --IS TO MAKE CHANGES -
IT IS A "NEW" AND EASY METHOD
TO PROMOTE RESEARCH
AND
INCREASE A NATION'S WEALTH AND HEALTH

FIRES
FIRST AID
FIRST AID & EMERGENCIES

FISH OILS IN HEALTH & DISEASE
FISHES (TILAPIA)
FLOWMETERS (RHEOLOGY)
FLUOXETINE (PROZAC, ET)

FOOD & DIET: HARMFUL REPORTS, ILL, CANCER
FOOD & ITS DANGEROUS INGREDIENTS
FOOD ADDITIVES
FOOD ADDITIVES: HARMFUL REACTIONS, ETC
FOOD--CALORIE INTAKE & EFFECTS

FOOD COLORING AGENTS & TOXICITY
FOOD CONTAMINATION
FOOD DISPENSERS & VENDING MACHINES
FOOD HABITS AND CUSTOMS
FOOD IRRADIATION
FOOD MANIA AND OVER-EATING
FOOD SWEETENERS -ASPARTAME & ADVERSE R
FOOD VALUES & BIOAVAILABILITY

FOOT CARE & RESEARCH

FOOTBALL
FORECASTING
FOUNDATIONS: GOALS & ROLES
FRACTURES

FRAUD, MALPRACTICE, PRETENSE, DECEPTION
FUTUROLOGY
GARLIC: MEDICAL & HEALTH QUALITIES
GASOLINE
GASTRO-INTESTINAL DISEASES

GENEALOGY & RELATIVE FACTORS
GENETIC ENGINEERING & CELL INTERVENTION
GENETIC SCREENING
GENETIC TOXICITY TESTS
GENOME BIOLOGY

NEW REFERENCE BOOKS & RESEARCH INDEXES

RESEARCH IS THE MOST UN-DEVELOPED THEME IN ALL NATIONS --
WHAT A TRAGEDY!

GERIATRICS & MEDICINE

GINSENG -IN LIFE & HEALTH
GLASS & GLASSOIDS

GLAUCOMA

GOLD -STUDIES & USES
GOVERNMENTS & AGENCIES: ACTIVITIES & INFORMATION
GROWTH SUBSTANCES
GUIDEBOOK & REF: MED COMPUTERS

GUNS & FIREARMS: MEDICAL, PSYCHOLOGIC, LEGAL IML
GUNS, THE CONSUMER & ANTI-GUN COHORTS
GUNS, FIREARMS, CRIME & CONTROVERSY
GUNS, THE N.R.A. & CONSUMERS ARMED
GUNSHOT WOUNDS IN CRIME & MED
GYMNASTICS & VARIATIONS

HAIR ANALYSIS

HAND INJURIES
HANDICAPPED & THE DISABLED

HAZARDOUS SUBSTANCES IN HEALTH, BEHAV, INDUSTRY

HEAD & NECK CANCERS
HEAD INJURIES

HEALTH & BIO-SCIENCE AWARDS, PRIZES
HEALTH & LIFE HAZARDS
HEALTH & MED ASPECTS: CHEM INDUSTRIES
HEALTH & MED DIAGNOSTIC ERRORS: THERAPY & TREAT
HEALTH -DANGERS, RISKS AND ASSESSMENTS
HEALTH CARE FINANCING IN U.S.

HEALTH CARE REFORM: SPECIFICS, ECONOMICS, LEGISLAT

HEALTH CARE SERVICES IN PRISONS
HEALTH DANGERS IN OUR DRINKING WATER
HEALTH DOCTORS WITH IMPAIRMENTS, AIDS, ETC
HEALTH DOCTORS; VIEWS, WRITINGS, RIGHTS, ET
HEALTH EDUCATION

NEW REFERENCE BOOKS & RESEARCH INDEXES

RESEARCH REQUIRES A WELL-EDUCATED MIND AND SOMEONE WITH SOME CURIOSITY.

****ALL CITIZENS MUST TEACH POLITICIANS
THE IMPORTANCE
OF
RESEARCH FOR ALL PEOPLE

HEALTH HAZARDS, SKIN PROBLEMS BY WORK
HEALTH HAZARDS IN OCCUPATIONS

HEALTH INSURANCE FOR AGED & DISABLED: T18
HEALTH MAINTAIN ORG (HM0)
HEALTH POLICY FOR HIV INFECTION & AIDS
HEALTH POLICY WITH PLANS, PRIORITIES, P & P
HEALTH PRIORITIES IN THE U.S.A.
HEALTH PROGRAMS: SCOPE, STRAT,CRITIC & PRAC
HEALTH PROMOTION
HEALTH PROTECTION & IMPROVEMENTS BY ADVICE, ET
HEALTH RESEARCH

HEALTH RESORTS & MEDICINE
HEALTH SCIENCE DOCUMENTATIONS
HEALTH SCIENCES RESEARCH I
HEALTH SCIENTISTS BIBLE OF BIBLIOGRAPHY
HEALTH SCIENTISTS BIBLE OF BIBLIOGRAPHY

HEALTH STATUS INDICATORS
HEARING & HEARING DISORDERS
HEART ATTACKS & REHABILITATION
HEART ATTACKS: REAL, IMAGINED, SUSPICIOUS
HEART FUNCTION TESTS
HEART INJURIES
HEMODYNAMICS: DIRECTORY & REVIEWS INDEX

HEMORRHOIDS

HEPATITIS C: DIRECTORY & REVIEWS INDEX
HERNIA -SIMPLE & COMPLEX
HERPES GENITALIS

HISTORY OF MEDICINE
HISTORY OF PRISONS
HISTORY OF WAR
HIV TRACING & TRANSMISSION: WORK, SPORTS, ETC
HOLOCAUST

NEW REFERENCE BOOKS & RESEARCH INDEXES

RESEARCH HELPS ALL BABIES TO A HEALTHY BIRTH AND A THRIVING CHILDHOOD.

HOME CARE SERVICES
HOMELESS & STREET PEOPLE

HOMEOPATHY
HOMICIDE
HOMOSEXUALITY
HORMONE PHYSIOLOGY
HORMONES

HORSES
HOSPICE & TERMINAL CARE
HOSPITAL ECONOMICS

HOSPITAL INFECTIONS & PATIENTS
HOSPITAL INFECTIONS: PREVENTION & CONTROL
HOSPITALIZATION
HOSTILITY CHARACTERISTICS & BEHAV
HOTLINES: PURPOSE, SERV & NEEDS

HUMAN ABNORMALITIES CAUSED BY CHEM, DRUGS, ETC
HUMAN ABORTION
HUMAN BEHAVIOR & REACTIONS TO LIVING
HUMAN BEHAVIOR & SOCIAL CONTROL MANAGEMENT

HUMAN BEHAVIOR: ANALYSIS, THERAPY, TREATMENTS
HUMAN CONCEPTS OF LIFE, LOVE, WORK
HUMAN DESIRES & EXPECTATIONS OF FUTURE
HUMAN EXPERIMENTATION

HUMAN HEMORRHOIDS

HUMAN LIFE EXPECTANCY:EXPERIEN & ANAL
HUMAN LIVING AND HOW LIFE-EVENTS INFLUEN
HUMAN LONGEVITY: ANAL, INFLUENCE, RISKS, ETC
HUMAN MIND & BODY ACTIONS AT HOME, WORK, SPORTS
HUMAN OBESITY: TREATMENT & THERAPY
HUMAN PREGNANCY COMPLICATIONS

HUMAN PSYCHOLOGY OF SINGLE PERSON
HUMAN RIGHTS
HUMAN RIGHTS & JURISPRUDENCE
HUMAN RIGHTS & SOCIAL JUSTICE

NEW REFERENCE BOOKS & RESEARCH INDEXES

GRADUATE EDUCATION AND ITS RESEARCH IS A POTENTIAL CAULDRON OF CREATIVITY.

HUMAN RIGHTS TO DIE

HUMAN SEX BEHAVIOR
HUMAN STRESS & DISTRESS: PSY & MED THER
HUMAN STRESS & ESCAPE REACTIONS
HUNGER
HYDROXYBENZOIC ACIDS

HYPERTENSION
HYPNOSIS
HYPOGLYCEMIA
IATROGENIC DISEASES 1
IMMIGRATION & EMIGRATION
IMPOTENCE

INCEST: ACTS, MYTHS & FACTS

INDIANS OF NORTH AMERICA
INDUSTRY & HEALTH AFFAIRS

INFANT FOOD & NUTRITION OF NEWBORN
INFECTION & INFECTIONS
INFECTIONS BY HOOKWORMS
INFECTIOUS SKIN DISEASES
INFLAMMATION
INFORMATION SERVICES FOR THE WORLD
INFORMATION SYSTEMS
INJURIES & WOUNDS 1
INJURIES OF THE SPINAL CORD

INSOMNIA
INSTITUTIONALIZATION
INSURANCE & ECONOMIC VALUES OF LIFE
INSURANCE LIABILITY

INSURANCE LIABILITY & LEGAL IMPLICATIONS
INTELLIGENCE
INTELLIGENCE TESTS
INTERIOR DESIGN & FURNISHINGS
INTERNAL MEDICINE
INTL BIBLIOGRAPHY: CRIME PUBLICATIONS
INTL COOPERATION IN MED & SCIENCE

NEW REFERENCE BOOKS & RESEARCH INDEXES

RESEARCH KEEPS WORMS AND MANY TYPES OF PARASITES OUT OF OUR BODIES.

INTERNSHIP & RESIDENCY
INTERPERSONAL RELATIONS

INTRA-UTERINE DEVICES
INVERTEBRATES

JEWS & ETHNIC FACTORS
JEWS, JUDAISM & THE HOLOCAUST

JURISPRUDENCE
JURISPRUDENCE & ASBESTOS
JURISPRUDENCE & CHILD ABUSE PREVENTION
JURISPRUDENCE & CLINICAL COMPETENCE
JURISPRUDENCE & CONFIDENTIALITY

JURISPRUDENCE & CONSUMER PRODUCT SAFETY
JURISPRUDENCE & CRIME
JURISPRUDENCE & CRIME ANALYSIS

JURISPRUDENCE & DIAGNOSTIC ERRORS

JURISPRUDENCE & DOCTOR-CAUSED DISEASES
JURISPRUDENCE & DRUG-NARCOTIC CONTROL
JURISPRUDENCE & EXPERT TESTIMONY
JURISPRUDENCE & FORENSIC TECHNOLOGY
JURISPRUDENCE & FORENSICS
JURISPRUDENCE & GOVERNMENT FINANCING
JURISPRUDENCE & HIV INFECTED CARE PERSONNEL

JURISPRUDENCE & WRONGFUL BIRTHS, NEGLIGENCE
JURISPRUDENCE & IATROGENIC (DOCTOR) PROBLEMS
JURISPRUDENCE & INFORMED CONSENT
JURISPRUDENCE & INSURANCE LIABILITY
JURISPRUDENCE & LIFE SUPPORT CARE
JURISPRUDENCE & MED EQUIPMENT SAFETY & FAIL
JURISPRUDENCE & MEDICAL MALPRACTICE

JURISPRUDENCE & MEDICAL MISTAKES
JURISPRUDENCE & MEDICATION ERRORS
JURISPRUDENCE & OCCUPATIONAL HEALTH
JURISPRUDENCE & ORGAN PROCUREMENTS

NEW REFERENCE BOOKS & RESEARCH INDEXES

MANY OF US TODAY WOULD NOT BE ALIVE
BUT
FOR RESEARCH MADE ON
ANTIBIOTICS.

JURISPRUDENCE & PATIENT ADVOCACY
JURISPRUDENCE & RIGHTS TO TREATMENT
JURISPRUDENCE & SUBSTANCE ABUSE DETECTION
JURISPRUDENCE & HEALTH SCIENCES
JURISPRUDENCE & TRUTH DISCLOSURES
JURISPRUDENCE IN HEALTH AFFAIRS

JURISPRUDENCE IN HEALTH BIOLOGY
JURISPRUDENCE, AIDS, HIV & TRUTH DISCLOSURES
JURISPRUDENCE, MED RECORDS & SYSTEMS

JURISPRUDENCE, PRODUCT SAFETY & LIABILITY
JURISPRUDENCE, RIGHTS TO TREATMENTS IN PRISON
JUVENILE DELINQUENCY

JURISPRUDENCE & PATIENT ADVOCACY
JURISPRUDENCE & RIGHTS TO TREATMENT
JURISPRUDENCE & SUBSTANCE ABUSE DETECTION
JURISPRUDENCE & HEALTH SCIENCES
JURISPRUDENCE & TRUTH DISCLOSURES
JURISPRUDENCE IN HEALTH AFFAIRS

KIDNEY TRANSPLANTATION
KNEE INJURIES

LABOR IN PREGNANCY
LABORATORY DIAGNOSIS

LANGUAGE & ITS FORMS AT WORK & PLAY USA

LASERS IN MED, SCIENCE & BIOLOGY
LEARNING DISORDERS
LEG INJURIES

LEGAL & MED LIABILITY IN HEALTH SCIENCES
LEGAL LIABILITY & MALPRACTICE IN HEALTH SCIENCE
LEGISLATION IN HEALTH SCIENCES
LEPROSY

LESBIANISM

LIBRARIES

NEW RESEARCH BOOKS & RESEARCH INDEXES

OH !! DEVELOPMENT OF A NATION
 CAN BE MEASURED
 BY THE AMOUNT OF
 RESEARCH
  THEY PRODUCE.

LIBRARIES IN HEALTH SERVICE
LICE & PEDICULOSIS

LIFE CHANGE EVENTS & HEALTH
LIPIDS
LITHIUM IN BIOLOGY & MEDICINE
LIVER DISEASES

LOVE & LIBIDO
LUMBAR VERTEBRAE & INJURIES
LUNG DISEASES

MAGIC, SUPERSTITIONS & FOLKLORE
MALARIA
MALOCCLUSION

MALPRACTICE I
MALPRACTICE II
MALPRACTICE IN HEALTH OCCUPATIONS

MAMMOGRAPHY IN HEALTH & MEDICINE
MAMMOGRAPHY OF THE BREAST
MANAGEMENT OF PERSONNEL IN HEALTH SCIENCE
MARINE BIOLOGY
MARRIAGE & MARITAL THERAPY
MARRIAGE THERAPY
MARRIAGE ANALYSIS, TREATMENT & RESULTS

MASSAGE
MATERIAL TESTING & BIOCOMPATIBILITY

MEAT & HEALTH

MEDICAL & HEALTH BUSINESS & COMPETITION
MEDICAL & HEALTH COSTS OF CARE, ILLNESS, ET
MEDICAL & HEALTH PRACTICES: DEFENSIVE MED
MEDICAL & LEGAL LIABILITY IN HEALTH SCIENCE
MEDICAL & PSYCHOLOGICAL STRESS
MED-PSY OF PERSUASIVE COMMUNICATION

MED REPORTS: EFFICIENCY & PERFORMANCE
MEDICAL (ABBE) TRIBULATIONS, SABOTAGE, MURDER

NEW REFERENCE BOOKS & RESEARCH INDEXES

PEOPLE DIE EARLIER IN NATIONS THAT PRODUCE LESS RESEARCH THAN OTHER NATIONS.

ATTEMPT OF AUTHORS, LOSS OF SHIPMENTS, SURVEILLANCE & POISONINGS
MEDICAL ANALYSIS & REVIEWS OF HIV
MEDICAL ART OF RELAXATION IN SICKNESS & H

MEDICAL ASPECTS; FOOD HANDLING
MEDICAL ASSISTANCE: TITLE 19

MEDICAL CARE OF POOR & INDIGENT
MEDICAL CATHETERS & CATHERIZATIONS: HARM, ERRORS, PUNCTURES, MIGRATIONS DISPLACEMENTS & COMPLICATIONS

MEDICAL CAUSES OF DEATHS IN HOSPITALS

MEDICAL CONSULTATIONS; PRACTICE, IMPORTANCE

MEDICAL DANGERS IN OUR DRINKING WATER
MEDICAL: DECISIONS: AS 'DO NOT RESUSCITATE'
MEDICAL DEVICES
MEDICAL DEVICES & EQUIP: FAILURE, CONTAMINATION
MEDICAL ECONOMICS
MEDICAL EDUCATION
MEDICAL EFFECTS OF FREE RADICALS
MEDICAL ELECTRONICS & INSTRUMENTATION

MEDICAL EMERGENCIES
MEDICAL ETHICS
MEDICAL GRADUATES OF FOREIGN NATIONS
MEDICAL HEALTH OF THE WORLD

MEDICAL HISTORY
MEDICAL HISTORY OF CURRENT, OLD WARS
MEDICAL IMITATIONS OF ILLNESS, PRETENSE
MEDICAL INDEX OF SEVERITY OF SICKNESS
MEDICAL JURIS & CRIMINAL LAW

MEDICAL JURIS & CRIMINAL LAW II
MEDICAL LIBRARIES; ROLES, CHALLENGES
MEDICAL MANUSCRIPTS, ANCIENT & MODERN
MEDICAL MASS SCREENING FOR H & DISEASE
MEDICAL MEASUREMENTS OF PAIN

NEW REFERENCE BOOKS & RESEARCH INDEXES

THE BEST STUDENTS AND CREATIVE MINDS COME FROM TEACHING TYPES OF SCIENTISTS.

MEDICAL PERIODICALS: FUNCTIONS, STANDARDS

MEDICAL PHYSICIAN IMPAIRMENTS
MEDICAL POLITICS
MEDICAL PRACTICE, DEFENSE MED, LEGAL ISSUES

MEDICAL PRESCRIPTIONS; ABUSE, EVAL, HABITS
MED PSEC OF ALCOHOL DRINKING ADDICTION

MED PSEC OF CHARACTER & PERSONALITIES
MED PSEC OF HOMOSEXUALITY, MALE, FEMALE
MED PSEC OF PHYSICIANS
MED PSEC OF REGRESSION & FACE PERSONALITY
MED PSYCHOLOGY OF SPOUSE ABUSE
MED PSYCHOLOGY OF ID, EGO & SUPEREGO
MEDICAL PSYCHOSOMATIC

MED REACTION, TREATMENT " OVERDOSE SUBSTANCES
MEDICAL REFERRALS FOR PACT & BUSINESS
MED RESEARCH & JUNGLE OF SCIENCE: NEW SYSTEM
MED RESEARCH IN HEALTH SCIENCES

MEDICAL RESEARCH: NEW CATEGORY: OXIDATIVE STRESS
MEDICAL RESEARCH: NEW CATEGORY: OXIDANTS
MED RESEARCH OF COMBAT DISORDERS, DAG, PSEC
MED RESEARCH OF CURRENT, PAST WARS
MED RESEARCH ON RADON & CANCER

MED RESEARCH ON STUDENTS

MED RESEARCH SUPPORT: WHAT'S GOING ON IN U.S.A.
MEDICAL SCHOOLS: ACTIVITIES, TRENDS, PROGRESS
MED SCIENCE APPLIED TO CRIME MYSTERY

MED SCIENTISTS R ON WAR & WARS: HISTORIC OPERATED

MED STUDIES OF HALLUCINOGENS
MED STUDIES OF POLYGRAPHS & OTHER LIE DETECTORS

MED STUDIES OF SALIVA
MED SUB ANAL: GENERAL COUNSELING
MED SUB RES: IATROGENESIS & IATROGENIC DISEASES

NEW REFERENCE BOOKS & RESEARCH INDEXES

COLLEGES HAVE BETTER RATINGS WHEN THEY HAVE PRODUCTIVE RESEARCH SCIENTISTS.

MED SUBJ RES: MED MALPRACTICE EXCLUD IATROLOGY

MED SUBJ RES CONCERNING COCAINE
MED SUBJ DIR & BIBL FOR PSYCHOSOMATIC MEDICINE

MEDICAL SYSTEMS ANALYSIS & MANAGEMENT
MEDICAL TECHNOLOGY
MED TREATMENT OF SELF & HYPOCHONDRIA

MED USES OF ANTIOXIDANTS FOR CANCER PREVENTION

MEDICAL WIT AND HUMOR
MEDICAL FACTORS IN HUMAN PERSONALITY DISORDERS
MEDICINE, PSEC & SCI IN AUTOMOBILE DRIVING

MENOPAUSE
MENSTRUATION DISORDERS

MENTAL & INTELLIGENCE TESTS
MENTAL DISORDERS
MENTAL FATIGUE -ANALYSIS, TESTS, ETC
MENTAL HEALTH
MENTAL HEALTH CARE IN PRISONS
MENTAL HEALTH SERVICES
MENTAL PROCESSES

MENTAL RETARDATION
METABOLISM WITH INBORN ERRORS

METALLURGY IN MED & INDUSTRY

METALS IN HEALTH, FOOD & POLLUTION

METALS-PHYSIOLOGY & METABOLISM

METEOROLOGY & WEATHER FACTORS
METHODS & INSTRUMENTATION FOR MED AUTOMAT
METHODS IN BEHAVIOR THERAPY

METHODS IN HYPNOSIS
MICROWAVES & RADIATION
MIGRAINE

NEW REFERENCE BOOKS & RESEARCH INDEXES

WITHOUT NEW RESEARCH WE WOULD LOSE DEVELOPMENTS OF THE LAST 500 YEARS.

MILITARY MEDICINE
MILK & MILK RESEARCH
MINERALS IN HEALTH, SCI & RESEARCH
MINN MULTI-PHASE PERSONALITY INVENTORY (MMPI)

MINOXIDIL (ROGAINE)
MMPI
MOLECULAR BIOLOGY IN HEALTH SCI

MORALE IN HEALTH, LIFE & WORK
MORALS & ISSUES

MULTIPLE SCLEROSIS
MUSCLE CONTRACTION
MUSCLES & DRUG EFFECTS
MUSCLES & PHYSIOLOGY

MUSIC, MUSICIANS & HEALTH INFLUENCES

MUTAGENS & MUTAGENICITY TESTS
MYCOSES
MYOCARDIAL INFARCTION WITH DIAGNOS
NEOPLASMS - PREVENTION & CONTROL
NEUROLOGY
NEURONS
NEUROTIC DISORDERS
NICOTINE

NOISE & ADVERSE EFFECTS ON HEALTH
NUCLEAR WARFARE
NURSE PRACTITIONERS
NUTRITION & MEDICINE
NUTRITION DISORDERS

NUTRITIONAL CONDITIONS: GOOD, BAD, DISEASED

OBESITY
OCCUPATIONAL DISEASES
OCCUPATIONAL MEDICINE

ONCOGENES
OPTOMETRY

NEW REFERENCE BOOKS & RESEARCH INDEXES

RESEARCH SCIENTISTS SEEK THE HOLY GRAIL OF PERFECTION FOR ALL MANKIND.

ORAL HEALTH & HYGIENE
ORGAN DONATIONS & PROCUREMENTS
ORTHOPEDICS
ORTHOPSYCHIATRY
OSTEOPATHY
OSTEOPOROSIS
OSTEOPOROSIS -CONDITIONS & THERAPY

PACEMAKERS
PARAPSYCHOLOGY & CLAIRVOYANCE
PARKINSONISM & TARDIV DYSKINESIA
PATENTS & HEALTH SCIENCE

PATHOLOGY
PATIENTS
PEDIGREE STUDIES

PEDOPHILIA & SEX BEHAVIORS

PEPTIDES
PERCHLORETHYLENE (DRYCLEANER, ET)
PERIODONTAL DISEASES
PERIPHERAL NERVE INJURIES
PERSONALITY DISORDERS

PERSONALITY TESTS & INVENTORY
PERSONNEL MANAGEMENT

PESTICIDES
PESTICIDES & CANCER
PETROLEUM & MEDICINE

PETS & DOMESTIC ANIMALS
PHENOLS & MEDICINE
PHENYTOIN (DILANTIN)
PHILATELY & HEALTH SCIENCE
PHILOSOPHY IN MED, SCI & HEALTH

PHOBIAS & DISORDERS
PHOTOGRAPHY IN LIFE SCIENCE
PHYSICAL EDUCATION & TRAINING
PHYSICAL ENDURANCE

NEW REFERENCE BOOKS & RESEARCH INDEXES

WHEN YOU HELP PROMOTE RESEARCH –

YOU HELP PROTECT YOUR FUTURE HEALTH.

PHYSICAL FITNESS
PHYSICAL FITNESS & SPORTS MED
PHYSICAL THERAPY & HEALTH

PHYSICIAN--PATIENT RELATIONS
PLASTICS IN MEDICINE, SCIENCE, LAW
PODIATRY
POISONING & MED

POLICE -HEALTH, RISKS, WORK, ET

POLITICAL SYSTEMS -PROG, REACT
POLITICS & BIOMEDICINE
POLYMERASE CHAIN REAC
POPULATION: CONTROL, SURVEILLANCE
POVERTY & CULTURAL DEPRIVATION
PREGNANCY: CARE & PHYSIOLOGY
PREJUDICE

PREMENSTRUAL SYNDROME
PREVENTIVE MEDICINE

PRISONERS
PRISONS
PROSTATE & MALE HEALTH
PROSTATE RESEARCH
PROTECTIVE DEVICES FOR SPORT & WORK

PROVERBS TWISTED WITH WIT & HUMOR
PROZAC (FLUOXETINE) SIDE EFFECTS
PSYCHIATRIC MODELS IN MED
PSYCHIATRIC NURSING

PSYCHIATRIC STATUS RATING SCALES
PSYCHIATRY & MEDICINE
PSYCHO-PHYSIOLOGIC DISORDERS
PSYCHO-PHYSIOLOGIC DISORDERS II
PSYCHO-PHYSIOLOGY & BIOFEEDBACK
PSYCHO-PHYSIOLOGY OF FATIGUE

PSYCHOLOGICAL ADAPTATION IN LIFE & WORK
PSYCHOLOGICAL DEPRIVATION

NEW REFERENCE BOOKS & RESEARCH INDEXES

*READING RESEARCH REVIEWS OF A SUBJECT GIVES YOU DECADES OF PROGRESS AND ADVANCEMENTS.

PSYCHOL IMPROVEMENTS WITH FOREIGN WORDS

PSYCHOLOGICAL TESTS

PSYCHOLOGICAL TESTS & TESTING
PSYCHOLOGY & A.I.D.S.

PSYCHOLOGY AND HEALTH
PSYCHOLOGY & ITS PRACTICE
PSYCHOLOGY & RESEARCH OF SELF CONCEPTS
PSYCHOLOGY & MED OF APPETITE DISORDERS

PSYCHOLOGY OF ALCOHOLISM

PSYCHOLOGY OF ANXIETY, WORRY, ETC
PSYCHOLOGY OF ATTACHMENT & BONDING

PSYCHOLOGY OF ATTEMPTED SUICIDE
PSYCHOL OF CORONARY & CARDIO-VAS DIS
PSYCHOLOGY OF HYPERTENSION
PSYCHOLOGY OF INDIANS OF N AMERICA
PSYCHOLOGY OF MENTAL DISORDERS

PSYCHOLOGY OF PAIN
PSYCHOLOGY OF PERCEPTIONS

PSYCHOLOGY OF SELF-AFFIRM & ASSERTIVENESS
PSYCHOLOGY OF STRESS & DISTRESS
PSYCHOLOGY OF TEMPERAMENT

PSYCHOLOGY OF FAMILY IN HEALTH, STRESS & DISEASE

PSYCHOLOGY OF WOMEN
PSYCHOLOGY, PARA-PSYCHOLOGY & CLAIRVOYANCE
PSYCHOMOTOR PERFORMANCES
PSYCHOTHERAPY

PUBLIC & SOCIAL POLICY
PUBLIC HEALTH
PUBLIC HEALTH: ADVANCES, PROBLEMS, RISKS, ET
PUBLIC HOUSING
PUBLIC OPINIONS YOU SHOULD KNOW ABOUT

NEW REFERENCE BOOKS & RESEARCH INDEXES

CREATIVITY REQUIRES THE CONSTANT FEEDING OF NEW KNOWLEDGE: MOSTLY, FROM RESEARCH

PUBLISHING IN THE LIFE SCIENCES: INDEX
PUBLISHING STANDARDS IN LIFE SCIENCE

PUBLISHING & SELLING YOUR OWN BOOK

PUNISHMENT: FORMS, FUNCTION, TRIALS, ET
QUALITY OF HEALTH CARE
QUESTIONNAIRES
QUESTIONNAIRES IN BIO-MED
RADIO & RADIO WAVES
RADIOTHERAPY
RADON

RAPE --HOW TO FIGHT, PREVENT, USE PROTECTIVE
　　　PSYCHOLOGY OR LATER IDENTIFY RAPIST

RAPE
RAPE & VIOLENCE
RAPE VICTIMS, OFFENDERS, TREATMENT, JURIS
RECENT ADVANCES IN COMPUTER SCIENCE

RED CROSS: GOALS & ROLES
REDUCING DIET
REFLEX & REFLEXES
REFUSE & GARBAGE DISPOSAL

REHABILITATION
RELAXATION TECHNIQUES

RELIGION & MEDICINE
RELIGION & PASTORAL CARE
RELIGION & PSYCHOLOGY
RELIGION & THE HIV-AIDS COMMUNITY
RELIGION WITH MED, PSY & PHILOSOPHY ASPEC
RELIGIOUS BELIEFS
REPRODUCTION

RESEARCH ON HEALTH
RESPIRATORY INSUFFICIENCY & THER
RESPIRATORY TRACT INFECTIONS

RESTAURANTS; CONDITIONS, SYNDROMES

NEW REFERENCE BOOKS & RESEARCH INDEXES

PEOPLE WITHOUT RESEARCH KNOWLEDGE ARE SELDOM THE BEST TEACHERS.

RESUSCITATION

RUNNING
SARCOMAS
SCHIZOPHRENIA
SCHIZOPHRENIC PSYCHOLOGY

SCHOOLS--PROGRESS, ACTIVITIES & TRENDS

SCIENCE & MED OF AUTOPSY
SCIENCE & MED OF BACKACHE
SCIENCE & MED OF SPORTS
SCI, MED & PSYCHOLOGY OF AUTOMOBILES
SCI, MED & PSYCHOLOGY OF PERSONALITY
SCLEROSIS
SCOLIOSIS

SEASONS AND ITS WEATHER, VAR & MOOD PSYCHOL

SEAT BELTS
SECURITY MEASURES
SEEDS
SELENIUM
SELF HELP GROUPS
SEMICONDUCTORS
SEPTICEMIA

SEX & BISEXUALITY
SEX & ORGASM RESEARCH
SEX & PEYRONIE'S DISEASE (PENILE)
SEX & PROSTITUTION
SEX & PSYCHOLOGY OF SEX OFFENSES
SEX & PSYCHOSEXUAL DEVELOPMENT

SEX & SEXUAL HARASSMENT

SEX & THE BIOLOGY OF COITUS
SEX & TRANSSEXUALISM
SEX BEHAVIOR
SEX BEHAVIOR, HIV & AIDS
SEX COUNSELING
SEX DISORDERS
SEX EDUCATION

NEW REFERENCE BOOKS & RESEARCH INDEXES

CREATIVITY REQUIRES
THE CONSTANT FEEDING
OF GOOD STUDENTS
WITH NEW KNOWLEDGE:
ESPECIALLY SO
FROM RESEARCH

SEX OFFENSES
SEX RESEARCH & MED I
SEXUAL ABUSE OF CHILDREN

SEXUAL DEVIATIONS & PARAPHILIAS
SEXUALLY TRANSMITTED DISEASES
SHOCK
SKIN INJURIES
SKULL FRACTURES

SLEEP RESEARCH & POLYSOMNOGRAPHY

SMOKING

SOAPS & SURF ACTIVE AGENTS
SOCIAL BEHAVIOR
SOCIAL BEHAVIOR & MED
SOCIAL DISCRIMINATION & PREJUDICE
SOCIAL INTER-PERSONAL INTERACTIONS
SOCIAL PERCEPTIONS, IMPRESSIONS, MENTAL ACTIONS
SOCIAL PSYCHOLOGY
SOCIAL SECURITY

SOCIAL VALUES
SOCIAL WORK & HEALTH SCIENCES

SODIUM GLUTAMATE (M.S.G.)
SODIUM HYPOCHLORITE: USES, IMPORTANCE

SOLVENTS, NEW, USED, HAZARDOUS
SOVIET MILITARY MEDICINE

SPACE FLIGHT
SPACE FLIGHT & AEROSPACE MEDICIN

SPEECH

SPORTS: RESEARCH & GUIDEBOOK
SPORTS: GUIDEBOOK FOR REF & RES
SPORTS: INDEX OF MODERN DEVELOPMENTS
SPORTS & ANABOLIC STEROIDS

NEW REFERENCE BOOKS & RESEARCH INDEXES

WHERE THERE IS LESS RESEARCH
THERE IS MORE SICKNESS,
GREATER SPREAD OF DISEASE
AND CONSTANT
POVERTY
AND
AN UNHAPPY POPULATION

SPORTS & ATHLETIC INJURIES
SPORTS & BLOOD PRESSURE
SPORTS & COMPETITIVE BEHAVIOR
SPORTS & HEART RATE
SPORTS & NEW EXERCISE RESEARCH

SPORTS & PSYCHO-PHYSIOLOGY

SPORTS & PSYCHOLOGICAL INFLUENCES

SPORTS - MENTAL HEALTH, PSYCHIC STRESS, EMOTIONAL REACTIONS
SPORTS -PERFORMANCE & CIRCADIAN RHYTHMS
SPORTS PERFORMANCE: ANALYSIS, SKILLS, TRNG, ET

SPORTS REPORT: BASEBALL
SPORTS REPORT: FOOTBALL
SPORTS REPORT: SOCCER
SPORTS REPORT: SWIMMING

SPORTS REPORT: TENNIS
SPORTS REPORT: TENNIS ELBOW
SPORTS REPORT: TRACK & FIELD
SPORTS WITH RACQUETS (BADMINTON, RACQUETBALL & SQUASH)

SPORTS, DRUGS & DOPING

SPORTS, EXERCISE & ENERGY METABOLISM IN MEN AND WOMEN
SPORTS; PREVENTION, CONTROL OF ATHLETE INJURIES
STAMPS & PHILATELY HONORS IN SCI & MED

STERILIZATION & DISINFECTION
STRESS
STRESS DISORDERS IN POST-TRAUMA
SUDDEN DEATH

SUICIDE
SUICIDE & ITS PSYCHOLOGICAL INFLUENCES
SUICIDE PREVENTION & CONTROL
SUICIDE WITH ASSISTANCE

NEW REFERENCE BOOKS & RESEARCH INDEXES

RESEARCH IS SO IMPORTANT IT SHOULD BE MADE A UNIVERSAL LAW FOR ALL UNIVERSITIES, STUDENTS, TEACHERS AND FACULTIES.

SURGERY
SWIMMING

TEACHING: ACTIONS, METHODS, ETC
TECHNOLOGY ASSESSMENTS

TELECOMMUNICATIONS

TELEVISION IN MED & SCIENCE

TERATOGENS
THERAPEUTIC MATERIALS
THERAPEUTIC USES ANTI-OXIDANTS FOR HEALTH
    IMPROVEMTS
THERAPY MADE EASY WITH COMPUTER ASSIST

THERAPY OF ALCOHOLISM
THERAPY OF ANXIETY & CHRONIC WORRY

THERAPY OF MENTAL DISORDERS
THROMBOSIS
TISSUE DONATIONS & POST-M GIFTS
TOBACCO

TOBACCO SMOKE IN ACTIVE & PASSIVE POLLUTION

TOURETTE'S SYNDROME

TOXIC SUBSTANCES IN HEALTH BIOL
TOXICOLOGY I

TRACE ELEMENTS IN HEALTH BIOL

TRAFFIC ACCIDENTS
TRANQUILIZING AGENTS, ADVERSE EFFECTS
TRAVEL -BENEFITS & DANGERS, RISKS, WARNINGS, ET
TRETINOIN: ACTIONS, HARMFUL REACTIONS

TYPE A PERSONALITY   U.S.
CENTERS FOR DISEASE CONTROL

NEW REFERENCE BOOKS AND RESEARCH INDEXES

ALL NATIONS HAVE MANY SINS:
ONE SUCH:
POOR TEACHING EVERYWHERE
AND LACK
OF
THOROUGH TRAINING OF STUDENTS.

U.S. FOOD & DRUG ADMINISTRATION
ULTRASONIC DIAGNOSIS
ULTRAVIOLET RAYS & ADVERSE EFFECT
UNIVERSITY MALPRACTICE: ESSAYS
URINALYSIS: METHODS, DIAGN, STD & ABUSE INJURY
URINE & POLYMEDICINE: GUIDEBOOK
URINE STUDIES IN LABS & PRACTICE

VAGINITIS
VASECTOMY

VEGETABLES & HEALTH SCIENCE
VEGETARIANISM
VENEREAL DISEASES
VETERANS: CASES, OUTCOMES, ET

VETERINARIANS' NEW RESEARCH BIBLE
VETERINARY MEDICINE
VETERINARIANS' NEW RESEARCH BIBLE

VIDEOS: USES, METHODS
VIOLENCE: PSYCHOLOGY, MED & LEGAL ASPECTS
VIRUS DISEASES
VIRUSES

VITAMIN DEFICIENCIES
VITAMIN P COMPLEX (BIOFLAVANOIDS)
VITAMINS
VITAMINS & MEDICINE

VOLUNTEER HEALTH AGENCIES & WORKERS

WAR: MEDICAL, PSYCHOL, SCIENTIFIC ANALYSIS
WAR WITH MILITARY & CIVIL ASPECTS
WEATHER, HEALTH & BIOMEDICAL ASPECTS
WECHSLER SCALES

WHIPLASH INJURIES

NEW REFERENCE BOOKS AND RESEARCH INDEXES

**WITHOUT STRICT DISCIPLINE IN SCHOOLS,
WARS,
DISEASE, POVERTY
AND
MASS IGNORANCE
WILL CONTINUE FOREVER....**

WOMEN & PELVIC INFLAMMATORY DIS
WOMEN & SPOUSE ABUSE
WOMEN & TAMPONS

WOMEN & THEIR LIFE-STYLES
WOMEN & VAGINA RESEARCH

WOMEN & WOMEN'S RIGHTS
WOMEN'S BIBLIOGRAPHY OF CONCERNS, ETC
WOMEN'S HEALTH SERVICES

WORK, INJURIES & COMPENSATION
WORK, JOBS, DISTRESS, DANGERS & DISEASE

WORKMAN'S COMPENSATION

WORLD HEALTH & THE W.H.O.
WOUND HEALING
YIN DEFICIENCY & YIN-YANG
YOGA
ZIDOVUDINE IN THERAPEUTIC USE

ZOONOSES & MEDICINE
ZYMONAS

BE AN EXPERT WITH ABBE INDEXES

<><><><><><><><><><><><><><><><>

ABBE INDEXES CONNECT YOU TO MANY FAMOUS PHYSICIANS, SCIENTISTS AND RESEARCH PIONEERS OF THIS WORLD.

<><><><><><><><><><><><><><><><>